WRITE IDEAS
A Beginning Writing Text

Connie Shoemaker and Susan Polycarpou

Spring International Language Center
Arapahoe Community College

HEINLE & HEINLE PUBLISHERS

A Division of Wadsworth, Inc.
Boston, Massachusetts 02116 U.S.A.

The publication of *Write Ideas* was directed by the members of the Newbury House Publishing Team at Heinle & Heinle:

Erik Gundersen, Editorial Director
Susan Mraz, Marketing Manager
Kristin Thalheimer, Production Editor

Also participating in the publication of this program were:

Publisher: Stanley J. Galek
Editorial Production Manager: Elizabeth Holthaus
Project Manager: Judy Keith
Associate Editor: Lynne Telson Barsky
Assistant Editor: Karen Hazar
Associate Marketing Manager: Donna Hamilton
Production Assistant: Maryellen Eschmann
Manufacturing Coordinator: Mary Beth Lynch
Photo Coordinator: Martha Leibs-Heckly
Page Layout: Christine E. Wilson, IBC
Interior Artist: Donna Stackhouse
Interior Designer: Nancy Lindgren Reid
Cover Illustrator: Jeanne Berg
Cover Design: Bortman Design Group

Shoemaker, Connie
    Write ideas / Connie Shoemaker and Susan Polycarpou.
        p.   cm.
    ISBN 0-8384-3987-X
    1. English language—Textbooks for foreign speakers.   2. English language—Rhetoric.   I. Polycarpou, Susan.   II. Title.
PE1128.S545   1993
428.2'4—dc20   93-27955
                                                        CIP

Heinle & Heinle is a division of Wadsworth, Inc.
Manufactured in the United States of America.

10 9 8 7 6 5 4 3

To Pambos and Floyd

Contents

WRITE IDEAS

Using the Steps to Describe Yourself

DESIGNING A T-SHIRT FOR YOURSELF

WRITING ABOUT YOURSELF

MAIN IDEA SENTENCES

THE SIMPLE PRESENT TENSE OF *TO BE*

Using the Steps to Describe Someone

DESCRIBING A PICTURE

WRITING TITLES

PUNCTUATING SENTENCES

Going the Extra Mile: Journal Writing

Using the Steps to Explain a Sport

TALKING ABOUT A PICTURE

MAKING A LIST

FINISHING A PARAGRAPH ON THE BOARD

Preface: *WRITE IDEAS:* A BEGINNING WRITING TEXT

Writing is a learnable and exciting process of creation for students at all levels of English. *Write Ideas* embodies this philosophy by guiding beginning level students through the steps of gathering ideas, focusing or forming a main idea, supporting, drafting, revising, editing, and drafting again

WHAT ARE THE DISTINCTIVE FEATURES OF *WRITE IDEAS?*

1. ***Writing as a recursive process.*** *Write Ideas* utilizes current second language writing research and applies it to the beginning writer. The book views writing as a recursive process that can be learned by the student. It offers exercises that encourage the student to generate ideas, focus on a main idea, support that idea, draft, revise, edit, and draft again.

   Revision and editing are treated as distinct tasks in the process, emphasizing the importance of meaning and clarity during revision and placing editing for grammar, punctuation, and spelling as a separate step. Revision and editing charts help students to know what to look for during these two steps in the process.

2. ***Writing as an experiential process.*** *Write Ideas* does more than simply describe the writing process. It allows students to *experience* the process as they progress through each chapter. Writing as a process becomes a natural part of

their language learning experience and provides the structure of good writing habits for future academic performance.

In the year and a half in which we classroom tested the material, we saw the effects of this approach as beginning level students successfully progressed through their writing classes to the advanced level.

3. **Integration of the four language skills.** The text encourages students to speak, listen, and read as they go through the writing steps. This process reinforces all skills and demonstrates that writing can be an interactive process.

4. **Writing from personal knowledge.** Many books at this level offer only assignments in copying based on model paragraphs or fill-in-the-blank exercises. This text encourages students who have limited English proficiency to write about topics in which they are interested. This is *each* student's individual writing, *not* a copy of a model paragraph.

5. **Contextualized approach to grammar instruction.** The writing exercises are designed to reinforce grammar and to give students the opportunity to use grammar in a natural context.

FOR WHOM IS THE BOOK DESIGNED?

Write Ideas is written for the beginning English as a second or foreign language student who is literate in his or her own language. It assumes that students have basic handwriting skills and beginning reading and spelling ability. The challenges it presents are suitable to students whose cognitive abilities are greater than their linguistic skills. As the book was being developed, it was classroom tested with level one of two five-level intensive English programs located on college and university campuses. Students in these two programs tested in the 25-37 point range of the Michigan Test of English Language Proficiency. *Write Ideas* is also quite suitable for high beginners in an adult education program.

HOW IS THE BOOK ORGANIZED?

Each chapter of *Write Ideas* opens with a photo of a real student and a brief passage describing an interesting aspect of that student's life. The passage uses the grammar points emphasized in the chapter and gives an initial example of the writing and grammar focus for that unit.

Students are then guided through the steps in the writing process: getting ideas (through the use of mapping, brainstorming, free writing, and oral work in pairs and groups), focusing and forming a main idea, supporting the main idea, drafting, revising and editing (through revision charts and peer work), and drafting again.

Grammar and punctuation are introduced in the order in which they are taught in most grammar texts. We believe that grammar at the beginning level is learned more by example than by explanation; thus, the discussions of grammar in the text are brief and to the point. They are intended mainly as a reference and reminder for the student.

Writing research shows that beginning ESL students tend to look only for grammar and punctuation errors and to neglect revision of content and ideas; hence, this text considers revision first, and as a separate entity, before focusing on editing. After revision, students consider grammar and punctuation explanations and related exercises while they are working on their first drafts.

At least two separate writing assignments are included in each chapter. Students progress from writing one paragraph in the early chapters to more extensive writing in later chapters. These assignments can be re-ordered if the instructor prefers to use one topic before another.

The conclusion of each chapter, "Going the Extra Mile," suggests topics for journal writing. An instructor who wishes to use the text for more than 9 to 12 weeks may wish to use the journal topics as extra writing assignments.

The Appendix includes handwriting guidelines, lists of commonly misspelled words and irregular past tense forms, a simplified chart of proofreading symbols, examples of ways to generate ideas, and a generic revision/editing chart, which may be used by students for extra assignments or by the instructor to determine a grade for the assignment.

Our own process of writing this text has been enriched by the support and encouragement of our colleagues at Spring International Language Center. Special thanks to those instructors who classroom tested the book at two centers of Spring: Arapahoe Community College and the Auraria Higher Education Center. We also wish to acknowledge the students who allowed us to use their photos and their stories to introduce each chapter.

C. S.
S. P.

INTRODUCTION TO THE WRITING PROCESS: *STEP BY STEP*

It is fun to climb a mountain, but it is not easy. If you take the right steps, you will get to the top of the mountain. You must get ideas about your climb, get ready to go, gather the things you need, and then start up the mountain. When you reach the top, you are not finished yet! You must come down the mountain, step by step.

Writing a paragraph is like climbing a mountain. Each step is important. You get some ideas and pick a main idea. Then you make your main idea stronger with other ideas that help it. Next you write everything down, but you are not finished yet! You must read your writing and make changes so that the reader will understand what you mean.

Steps in Writing a Composition

GETTING
IDEAS

FOCUSING ON A
MAIN IDEA

SUPPORTING THE
MAIN IDEA

DRAFTING

REVISING

EDITING

WRITING A
FINAL DRAFT

Example of Writing Process

GETTING IDEAS

My New Car

blue inside – outside
beutiful
I love her
buy her Jan. 2
Toyota Celca
smell lovely – new
soft seats
cost too much
I work for long time t
power window & locks

My New Car

blue inside – outside
beutiful
I love her
buy her Jan. 2
Toyota Celca
smell lovely – new
soft seats   music / tape
cost too much   big speekers
I work for long time to pay
power window & locks
She is my sweetheart.

FOCUSING

3

SUPPORTING

My New Car
She is my sweetheart

1. beutiful — fast
2. blue
3. soft seats
4. smell lovely
5. ~~buy her Jan. 2~~
6. nice music
7. Toyota Celca

DRAFTING

My New Car

My new car she is my sweetheart.
She is beutiful and fast. She has
blue color inside and outside. She
has soft seats and power windows
and locks and smell lovely. Also has
nice music from tape player. She has
to speekers in back. She is Toyota
Celica.

REVISING

My New Car

My new car she is my sweetheart. She is beutiful and fast. She h~~as~~ *is* blue c~~o~~lor inside and outside she has soft seats and power windows and locks and smell lovely. Also, ~~has~~ *she gives me* nice music from tape player. She has to speekers in back. *Her name* ~~She~~ ⟨is Toyota Celica⟩ I love my new car.

EDITING

My New Car

My new car s~~he~~ is my sweetheart. Her name is Toyota Celica. She is blue inside and outside. ~~h~~*S*he has soft seats and power windows and locks. a~~nd~~ *She* smells lovely. Also she gives me nice music from *a* tape player. She has ~~two~~ *a* spe~~a~~kers in back. I love my new car.

**DRAFTING
AGAIN**

John Calder
Writing 1
January 23

My New Car

My new car is my sweetheart. Her name is Toyota Celica. She is very beautiful and very fast. She is blue inside and outside. She has soft seats and power windows and locks. She smells lovely. Also, she gives me nice music from her tape player. She has two speakers in back. I love my new car.

WRITING IS LIKE A WHEEL

It can go forwards and backwards. You may finish steps one, two, and three. Then you may want to go back to step one and think of more ideas. That's OK. Use the steps as you need to, but finish all of them. If you go through all six steps, you will write a good paragraph.

LOOK AT THIS WHEEL. Write the names of the six steps on the lines of the wheel.

I think about what I am going to write. I write my ideas in a list, a web, or a chart.

I write it again. I make a neat copy.

I find a main idea.

I support my main idea with details and examples.

I make changes in grammar, punctuation, and spelling.

I read my paragraph and make changes in organization, words.

I write a first copy. I don't worry about perfect English.

WORDS YOU SHOULD KNOW

Heading	Your name, class, and the date
Title	The name you give to the composition
Indent	Empty space before a paragraph begins
Paragraph	A group of sentences about the same idea
Composition	More than one paragraph about a central idea
Sentence	A group of words with a subject and verb, starting with a capital letter and ending with a period, question mark, or exclamation point
Main Idea	What the paragraph is about (also called topic sentence)
Supporting Sentences	Details added to the topic sentence
Margin	Space on the left or right side of the paper
Skip Lines	Leave one space between lines
Conclusion	End of paragraph or composition

CAN YOU MATCH THE WRITING WORDS WITH THE PARAGRAPH THAT FOLLOWS? Write the letter from the paragraph next to the word.

_____ Title   _____ Main Idea

_____ Heading   _____ Margin

_____ Indent   _____ Conclusion

_____ Paragraph   _____ Sentence

Which words from the list are not here? Find them in the paragraph.

A John Calder
Writing 1
January 23

B My New Car

G My new car is my sweetheart. Her name is Toyota Celica. She is very beautiful and very fast. H She is blue inside and outside. She has soft seats and power windows and locks. She smells lovely. Also, she gives me nice music from her tape player. She has two speakers in back.

E I love my new car.

Journal Writing

The more you write, the better you will write. Writing each week in a journal will help you to write better. A journal is a special notebook in which you write about anything that interests you. Each chapter of this book also gives you ideas about what to write. You may wish to share what you write with your teacher or a friend.

Kyung Tae

Chapter 1

GETTING ACQUAINTED: *KYUNG TAE*

Do they play ice hockey in South Korea? They certainly do! Last year K.T. was a 15-year-old hockey star in Seoul, Korea. Now he is one of the stars of his beginning English class in the United States. He studies English 25 hours a week. He also plays hockey 15 hours a week.

He is short and very fast on ice skates. In school he likes to joke and laugh. His real name is Kyung Tae, but he calls himself K.T. It's easy for Americans to say. Video games and drawing are some of his favorite things, but ice hockey is his first love.

Using the Steps to Describe Yourself

◆ GETTING IDEAS

DESIGNING A T-SHIRT FOR YOURSELF

K.T. told his classmates about himself by drawing pictures and putting words on the outline of a T-shirt. Here is his T-shirt:

On the page that follows, make a T-shirt for yourself. Draw pictures and write words on the T-shirt. Then show your classmates the shirt and tell about yourself.

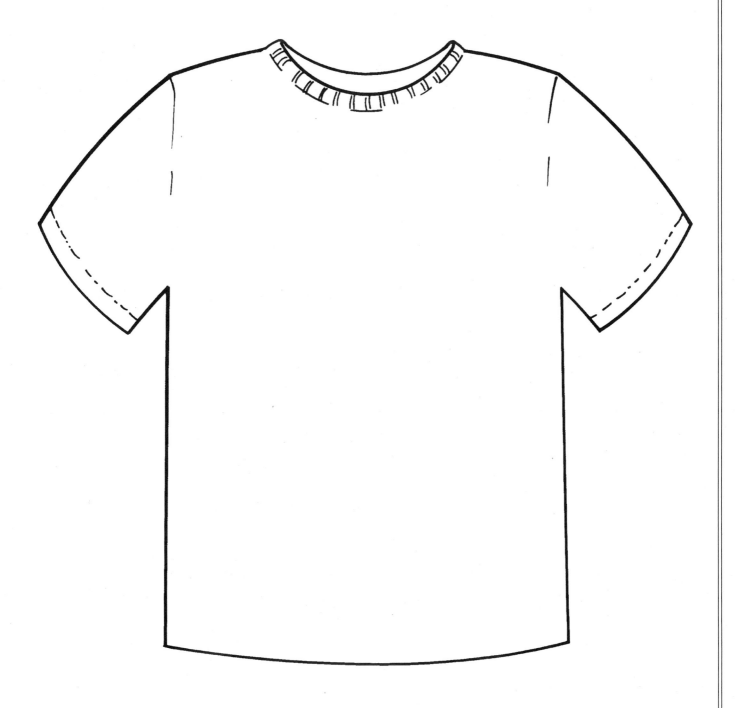

◆ FOCUSING AND SUPPORTING

WRITING ABOUT YOURSELF

Look at your t-shirt. Can you add more words that tell about yourself? Write all of the words that describe **you** on the list that follows:

What kind of person am I?   What do I like?

_____   _____

_____   _____

_____   _____

_____   _____

_____   _____

What are other things I want my classmates to know?

_____

_____

_____

Look at your list. What is the most important thing about you? Put a circle around it. Then write a sentence about it.

Main idea: _____.

Are there other words on your list that tell interesting or important things about you? Circle these words, too, and use them in your paragraph.

◆ DRAFTING

Now you're ready to write. Follow this plan to write a paragraph about yourself.

Who Am I?

Hello. My name is _____.

I am from _____. _____

_____

_____

_____

_____

_____

_____

_____

_____

_____

_____

_____

Now you know who I am. I hope we can become friends.

◆ REVISING

MAIN IDEA SENTENCES

A good composition has a main idea sentence that tells the reader what the composition is about.

Exercise 1.1. Finding the main idea. Read this paragraph and underline the sentence that you think tells the main idea. Talk about your choice with your classmates.

Who Am I?

My name is Natasha. I am from Switzerland. I love to ski. I learned to ski when I was five years old. In Switzerland, I ski every weekend with my father and my sister. When we have a winter vacation, we always go to the mountains to ski. I also train for skiing. I go to a gym three times a week. I exercise to be fit and to make my legs strong. Here in the U.S., I go to school to learn English, but I go skiing every weekend. Now you know what I like to do. I hope we can become friends.

REVISING YOUR COMPOSITION

Sit together with a classmate. Read your classmate's paragraph and have him or her read yours. Work together to answer these questions about your compositions. Check *yes* or *no*. Use your answers to help you make changes in your compositions.

ORGANIZATION, IDEAS	YES	NO
Is there a sentence that says something important about you?		
Do all the other sentences talk about interesting things about you?		
Is the paragraph at least eight sentences long?		

◆ EDITING

THE SIMPLE PRESENT TENSE OF *TO BE*

In English, the verb agrees with the subject of the sentence. Here are some sentences that use the simple present tense of the verb *to be.*

SUBJECT	*TO BE*	REST OF SENTENCE
I	am	a student.
You	are	a businessman.
He	is	from Egypt.
She	is	Japanese.
It	is	a new store.
We	are	students.
You	are	teachers.
They	are	doctors.

What is a subject? the person or thing that the sentence is about

Where is it in the sentence? usually before the verb, except in questions

What part of speech is a subject? a pronoun or noun and any words that modify it

Exercise 1.2. Finding subjects and verbs. Here are some sentences about K.T. Underline the subject in each of the sentences. The first one is done for you.

1. <u>K.T.</u> is a student.

2. He is from Korea.

3. Hockey is his favorite pastime.

4. Susan is his writing teacher.

5. Ten students are in his class.

6. The students are from many countries.

7. The classroom is in a new building.

8. The building is near the post office.

Now go back and circle the verb in each sentence. When do you use *is?* When do you use *are?*

Exercise 1.3. Using the correct form of the verb to be. Fill in each blank with a form of *to be*. The first one is done for you.

1. Mark _____*is*_____ my friend.

2. He and I _____ students in algebra class.

3. We _____ good students.

4. Our teacher _____ Carol Moore.

5. She _____ from New York and her husband _____, too.

6. They _____ New Yorkers, but they like it here in California.

7. _____ you from California, too?

8. It _____ a nice place to live.

MAKING SENTENCES WITH *TO BE*

SUBJECT	*TO BE*	REST OF SENTENCE
noun	am is are	adjective
or		
pronoun	am is are	adjective

Noun   a person, place, or thing *(Khaled, house, book)*

Pronoun   I, you, he, she, it, we, you, they

Adjective   a word that describes a noun *(tall, green, old)*

Exercise 1.4. Using nouns, pronouns, and adjectives.   Write a noun or pronoun in each blank.

1. _____*I*_____ am tall.

2. _____ and _____ are intelligent.

3. The _____ is blue.

4. The _____ are young.

5. _____ is pretty.

6. The _____ is good.

7. The _____ are green.

8. _____ are nice.

9. _____ is old.

10. _____ are tired.

Now write an adjective in each blank.

1. My mother is _____.

2. His grandmother and grandfather are _____.

3. The students in this class are _____.

4. You are _____.

5. This book is _____.

6. I am _____.

7. We are _____.

8. Omar is _____.

9. The weather is _____.

10. The cat is _____.

EDITING YOUR COMPOSITION

Use the questions in this chart to help you edit your paragraph.

GRAMMAR, PUNCTUATION, SPELLING, FORMAT	YES	NO
Is there a subject in each sentence?		
Are the forms of *be* correct?		
Does every sentence begin with a capital letter and end with a period?		
Are the words spelled correctly?		
Is the paragraph indented?		
Is there a heading (name, class, date)?		

◆ WRITING THE FINAL DRAFT

Make changes in your paragraph. Write the paragraph again on another piece of paper. Carefully follow the form on page 6 of the Introduction.

Using the Steps to Describe Someone

♦ GETTING IDEAS

DESCRIBING A PICTURE

K. T.'s friend, Tae San, likes to draw cartoons. This is his picture of a character called Kiki. Add some more words to the list to describe him, or make your own drawing and list words that describe it.

Head	Body
large, round	fat
tiny, bright eyes	thin neck
long, curly moustache	long, thin arms
_____	_____
_____	_____
_____	_____
_____	_____
_____	_____
_____	_____

◆ FOCUSING AND SUPPORTING

What can you say about how Kiki looks? Finish this main idea sentence:

Kiki is a little unusual, but I think he looks _____

_____.

Circle the ideas from your list that you can use to explain this main idea.

◆ DRAFTING

Now finish the paragraph and write a title for it.

_____

Kiki is my favorite character. He is a little unusual, but I think he looks _____

_____

_____

_____

_____

_____

_____

_____

_____

_____

_____

_____

_____

_____

_____

_____ Do you think _____, too?

◆ REVISING

WRITING TITLES

A title is a few words that tell what your paragraph is about. Titles are not full sentences, but the first word of a title is always capitalized. Also, the first letter of each word is capitalized, except for prepositions *(to, of, in, for...)*, conjunctions *(and, but...)*, and articles *(a, an, the)*. Here are some examples of titles for a paragraph about K.T.:

My New Friend from Korea

A Hockey Star in My Class

K.T. and His Favorite Things

Exercise 1.5. Finding mistakes in titles.   Each title has two mistakes in capitalization. Find the mistakes and correct them.

1. The day I lost My Passport

2. My home town

3. my hobbies

4. Skiing In The Swiss Mountains

5. My Grandmother And Her wisdom

6. My Favorite City In my Country

7. a New Life For Me

8. The Best Place In The World

9. A Monster From The Planet Mars

10. A trip I'll never Forget

REVISING YOUR OWN PARAGRAPH

Read your composition aloud. Ask your classmates to help you answer *yes* or *no* to these questions. Use your answers to help you revise your composition.

ORGANIZATION, IDEAS	YES	NO
Does your paragraph begin with a description of Kiki's head and then talk about his body?		
Do all of the sentences talk about how Kiki looks?		
Are there at least six sentences to describe him?		
Is the title correctly capitalized?		

◆ EDITING

PUNCTUATING SENTENCES

A sentence is a complete idea with a subject and a verb. A sentence begins with a capital letter and ends with a period.

Examples: Yusef is an artist.
Those students are late to class.

Exercise 1.6. Finding subjects and verbs. Underline the subjects and circle the verbs in these sentences. The first sentence is done for you.

The Importance of English

English (is) important. Many people speak English in many countries. It is the language of business. I am from Thailand. I speak Thai at home. I speak English at work. I work in a bank. People in the bank are American and British. I am happy with my English and Thai.

Exercise 1.7. Using capital letters and periods. Look for the sentences in the following paragraph. Put a capital letter at the beginning of each sentence and a period at the end.

My Friend from Japan

yoshi is a college student from Japan he is very handsome he is about 180 centimeters tall he is slender his arms and shoulders are strong he has a round face with dark brown eyes his moustache is thick and black his teeth are shiny and white yoshi is quite nice looking

EDITING YOUR PARAGRAPH

Use the questions in this chart to help you edit your paragraph.

GRAMMAR, PUNCTUATION, SPELLING, FORMAT	YES	NO
Is there a subject and verb in each sentence?		
Is the spelling correct?		
Is there a capital letter at the beginning of each sentence?		
Is there a period at the end of each sentence?		
Is there a heading (name, class, date)?		

♦ WRITING THE FINAL DRAFT

Make the necessary changes in your paragraph. Write it again on another piece of paper.

Going the Extra Mile: Journal Writing

1. Write a paragraph about a classmate. Get information from the T-shirt that your classmate made. Also ask him or her questions about what he likes to do.

2. Write a paragraph describing your instructor.

3. Write a paragraph about a famous person such as a TV or film star, a sports figure, or a government leader.

Mohamed

Chapter 2

FUN ACTIVITIES:
Mohamed

Mohamed is from the United Arab Emirates. He is studying at an American college now. He is very busy with his classes, but he makes time for his favorite sport, soccer. It reminds him of the good times he had in his country. There, he played on a national team. Here in the United States, he often plays soccer after school with his friends, and they sometimes play against teams from other schools.

Using the Steps to Explain a Sport

♦ GETTING IDEAS

TALKING ABOUT A PICTURE

Mohamed wants to write about a soccer game because his teacher and his classmates want to know more about the sport. First, he makes a picture of his team playing soccer.

Mohamed tells his classmates about his picture. They ask him questions. What other questions can they ask?

1. How many players are on each team?

2. What are the names of the teams?

3. <u>What is the man with the ball doing?</u> _____

4. _____

5. _____

6. _____

7. _____

8. _____

◆ FOCUSING

Now Mohamed needs to write a sentence that tells what his paragraph is about. Write a main idea sentence for him. Use these ideas: soccer, fun, interesting.

Main idea sentence: _____

_____

◆ SUPPORTING

MAKING A LIST

Look at the picture again. Use the answers to the questions you asked in the GETTING IDEAS section. Make a list of words that talk about the picture.

People	**What they are doing**
_____	_____
_____	_____
_____	_____
_____	_____
_____	_____
_____	_____
_____	_____

◆ DRAFTING

FINISHING A PARAGRAPH ON THE BOARD

Work with your class. Finish Mohamed's paragraph. Everyone in the class should suggest sentences. Ask one person in your group to record the paragraph on the board or on a large piece of paper.

An Interesting Game

Playing a soccer game is really fun. In the picture, my team is playing a team from another school. My team is called the Bears. My friend Ken is kicking the ball.

_____

_____

_____

_____

◆ REVISING

Ask someone in your group to read your paragraph from the blackboard or sheet aloud. Work together to answer these questions.

ORGANIZATION, IDEAS	YES	NO
Do all of your sentences talk about the soccer game?		
Do you need any more sentences to explain the picture?		
Do you want to change the order of any sentences?		
Do you have a conclusion, a sentence at the end that repeats the main idea?		

Use your answers to suggest changes, and ask your recorder to write these changes in the composition.

◆ EDITING

Now, you are ready to look for mistakes in your writing. Use these questions to help you find errors.

GRAMMAR, PUNCTUATION, SPELLING, FORMAT	YES	NO
Are all of the words correctly spelled?		
Does every sentence begin with a capital letter and end with a period?		
Does each important word of the title begin with a capital letter?		

Your recorder should correct any mistakes that you made in spelling, grammar, or punctuation.

Using the Steps to Describe Your Favorite Sport

◆ GETTING IDEAS

DRAWING A PICTURE

Now write a paragraph about your favorite game or sport. Draw a picture of your game. Write a few words about the picture.

◆ FOCUSING

WRITING ABOUT YOUR FAVORITE GAME OR SPORT

Write a sentence that tells the name of your sport and something about it.

_____

◆ SUPPORTING

Tell your classmates about the picture you drew. Answer their questions and add some more words to your list.

DRAFTING

Now write your paragraph. You can begin and end like this.

My Favorite Game

_____ is my favorite game because it is _____.

I drew a picture of _____. In the picture, _____

_____

_____

_____

_____

_____

_____

_____

_____

_____

_____.

I think _____ is a lot of fun.

◆ REVISING

SUPPORTING SENTENCES

A good paragraph has a main idea sentence, and it has enough supporting sentences to explain the main idea.

Exercise 2.1. Identifying supporting sentences. What is the main idea sentence in this paragraph? Underline it. Now find the supporting sentences and number them. The first one has been done for you.

Camel Racing

Camel racing is a very popular sport in Qatar because it is exciting and there are big prizes for the winner. In this picture my friend Aziz is racing his favorite camel. [1.]First, he is putting a number on the camel. Next, the camels are lining up to start the race. Now the camels are running around the track. One of the other camels is running very fast. It is in front of the rest. Now Aziz's camel is running faster. It is passing the one in front. The people in the crowd are very excited. They are shouting and jumping. Now Aziz's camel is crossing the finish line first! Aziz is winning a beautiful new sports car. It is a good day for him and his camel.

How many supporting sentences did you find?

REVISING YOUR PARAGRAPH

Read your paragraph about your favorite sport to a friend. Ask him or her to help you answer these questions. Make the necessary changes.

ORGANIZATION, IDEAS	YES	NO
Does your first sentence tell the name of your sport or game?		
Does it say something about the game?		
Are there at least six supporting sentences to explain your picture?		
Do all the sentences talk about your sport or game?		
Is there a sentence at the end that repeats the main idea?		

◆ EDITING

PRESENT CONTINUOUS TENSE

The present continuous talks about now. We make the present continuous with:

SUBJECT	*TO BE*	VERB
noun or pronoun	*is* *am* *are*	verb + *ing*

Examples: Mary *is eating* lunch now.
I *am smoking* a cigarette.
Joy and Kevin *are talking* about their classes.

Exercise 2.2. Making present continuous sentences. Add some more nouns or pronouns and verbs with *ing* to the chart.

SUBJECT	TO BE	VERB + ING
I	am	swimming
Maria	is	running
Ali	is	playing
Juanita	is	writing
He	is	working
_____	is	_____
_____	is	_____
You	are	_____
We	are	_____
Bill and Lee	are	_____
The children	are	_____
_____	are	_____

Exercise 2.3. Writing present continuous sentences. Use the words from the chart, or use your own words. Write some sentences with the present continuous.

1. Juanita is running.

2. _____

3. _____

4. _____

5. _____

6. _____

7. _____

8. _____

9. _____

10. _____

EDITING YOUR COMPOSITION

Now use the questions in this chart to help you correct errors in your own composition.

GRAMMAR, PUNCTUATION, SPELLING, FORMAT	YES	NO
Are the present continuous verbs correct?		
Does every sentence have a capital letter and a period?		
Are the words spelled correctly?		
Is the paragraph indented?		
Is there a title?		
Is there a heading (name, classs, date)?		

◆ WRITING THE FINAL DRAFT

After you correct your paragraph, write it again.

Using the Steps to Describe What Is Happening

◆ GETTING IDEAS

TALKING ABOUT WHAT PEOPLE ARE DOING

Put yourself in the picture on the next page. Draw yourself doing something in this picture of the park.

Talk about the picture with your partner. Finish the list of the people and their activities.

Couple

holding hands

sitting on a bench

talking

People on a blanket

having a picnic

eating sandwiches

_____

Baby

looking at flowers

laughing

talking

Baseball players

_____

_____

_____

Swimmer

_____

_____

_____

Girl on a bicycle

_____

_____

_____

_____

Mother

walking on the path

pushing a baby carriage

_____

Girl on the swing

_____

_____

_____

Ice cream man

_____

_____

_____

_____
(your name)

_____

_____

_____

_____

◆ FOCUSING AND SUPPORTING

Where are you and the other people? Are you having a good time?

Write a main idea sentence about the picture.

_____

What other things can you add to your list? Is anyone doing anything else? Can you add specific words to describe the people or the park?

◆ DRAFTING

Put your ideas into sentences. Begin your paragraph with a main idea sentence.

_____

_____

_____

_____

_____

_____

_____

_____

_____

All of the people are enjoying a sunny day in the park.

◆ REVISING

USING ADJECTIVES FOR DESCRIPTION

We can make a description interesting if we use adjectives to tell more about people and things. As you know, an adjective is a word like *tall* or *green*. We can place adjectives before a noun or after the verb *to be*.

	ADJECTIVE	NOUN	*TO BE*	ADJECTIVE
The	*green*	trees	are	*beautiful.*

	ADJECTIVE	NOUN			ADJECTIVE	NOUN
The	*little*	boys	are playing	with a	*big*	dog.

Exercise 2.4. Adding descriptive adjectives. Use the adjectives from this list. Add them to the following sentences. You may use the same adjective more than once.

green	cool	delicious	small	tall
yellow	old	happy	young	large
sweet	cold	beautiful	warm	sunny

1. A _____ girl is buying an ice cream cone.

2. The ice cream is _____.

3. A _____ woman is pushing a baby stroller.

4. The _____ baby is looking at the

   _____ flowers.

5. There is a _____ tree.

6. A _____ boy is swimming.

7. The water is _____.

8. A _____ couple is sitting on the bench.

REVISING YOUR OWN PARAGRAPH

Read your paragraph aloud. Is there anything you need to change? Use this checklist to help you.

ORGANIZATION, IDEAS	YES	NO
Is there a main idea?		
Does your paragraph talk about all of the people in the park?		
Are there adjectives to describe the park and the people?		
Do all of the sentences talk about the picture?		
Is there a conclusion?		

♦ EDITING

WORD ORDER IN SENTENCES

The correct order of the words in an English sentence is

SUBJECT	VERB	OBJECT OR COMPLEMENT
The boys	are playing	basketball.
My sister	is	beautiful.

Exercise 2.5. Putting words in the correct order. Put the groups of words in the correct order to make good sentences. Remember to use capital letters and periods.

1. is/very tall/the teacher

   _____

2. fast/that car/is

   _____

3. is catching/a fish/Joan

   _____

4. the boys/ice cream/are eating

   _____

5. seventy years old/is/my grandmother

   _____

6. Maria/a pretty dress/is wearing

   _____

7. in the pool/the little girls/are swimming

   _____

8. a young woman/her baby/is carrying

   _____

9. horses/the boys/are riding

_____

10. from Indonesia/my friend/is

_____

EDITING YOUR PARAGRAPH

Answer these questions about your paragraph. Use your answers to help you correct your grammar, spelling, and punctuation.

GRAMMAR, PUNCTUATION, SPELLING, FORMAT	YES	NO
Are the present continuous verbs correct?		
Are the words spelled correctly?		
Are the words in each sentence in the correct order?		
Does every sentence begin with a capital letter and end with a period?		
Is there a title?		
Is there a heading?		

◆ WRITING THE FINAL DRAFT

Write your paragraph again on a new piece of paper after you have made the necessary changes.

Going the Extra Mile: Journal Writing

1. Go to a busy place like a shopping center, a restaurant, or a bus stop. Look at the people there. Who are they? What are they doing? Follow the steps. Write a paragraph about what the people in this place are doing.

2. Watch a cartoon like Bugs Bunny on TV, or find one in the newspaper. Tell what the characters are doing.

3. Imagine that you are a reporter on TV. Tell about what is happening at an important sports event or festival in your country.

Silvia

Chapter 3

SPECIAL PLACES: *Silvia*

"O-o-oh! It's so nice to be home!" Silvia says. "The first thing I do when I get home from work is take off my shoes and turn on my music."

Silvia's apartment is very important to her. She works long hours at a restaurant and also goes to school. When she gets home, she enjoys everything in her little apartment. She sits in a chair by the stereo and looks around the living room. All of her favorite things are there. She looks at the wall hanging above the sofa. It is from Peru, her native country. She also looks at the photos of her family that are on the wall above the stereo. She smells the sweet flowers in the vase on the coffee table. "This room is my special place," she says.

Using the Steps to Describe a Room

◆ GETTING IDEAS

MAKING A DIAGRAM OF YOUR ROOM

Do you have a favorite room at home in your country? Is there a room that you really like here in the United States? Draw a picture. Use your picture to describe the room to another student.

My Favorite Room

Answer these questions about your room on the chart below.

What is your favorite room?	
Where is this room? (In your country? In your family home? Here?)	
What furniture is in the room?	
What color are the walls? Are there pictures on the walls?	
How many windows are in the room?	
Are there curtains or drapes on the windows? What can you see outside?	
Are there any special smells in this room? (flowers? smoke? perfume? cooking?)	
Why do you like this room?	

◆ FOCUSING

Write a main idea sentence naming your favorite room and telling why you like the room.

_____

_____

◆ SUPPORTING AND DRAFTING

Use this sentence as the first sentence of a paragraph that describes your room. Use your drawing to help you tell where the furniture, windows, and doors are. Use your chart for words that describe the room. As you write the first draft, finish with a conclusion that repeats the main idea.

My Favorite Room

My favorite room is _____

_____ because _____

_____

_____

_____

_____

_____

_____

_____

_____

_____

_____

_____

_____

_____

_____

_____

_____

_____

_____

SENTENCES THAT DO NOT BELONG

Exercise 3.1. Finding sentences that do not belong. Read this paragraph. Underline the main idea. Find two sentences that do not support the main idea. Cross out these sentences.

My Favorite Restaurant

Pepito's is my favorite restaurant because it has great food and the people are friendly. The food is always fresh and homemade. Sometimes the desserts are too sweet. The fajitas and burritos are always good because they are hot and spicy. Pepito's has nice decorations from Mexico. The owners, Joe and Lucy Romero, always say "hello" to me and ask about my family. This is really a nice restaurant.

REVISING YOUR OWN PARAGRAPH

Read your paragraph aloud. Then answer these questions about it. If you answer "no" to any of the questions, make changes in your paragraph.

ORGANIZATION, IDEAS	YES	NO
Is there a main idea that tells which room is the favorite and why?		
Do all of the other sentences tell about the room?		
Is there a final sentence that says the same idea as the first sentence?		

◆ EDITING

PREPOSITIONS OF PLACE

on	under	beside	inside of	in front of
in	above	between	on top of	in back of
outside of	next to	opposite	by	behind

Exercise 3.2. Using prepositions. Look at the picture and answer the questions using *there's*.

Example: What's on the coffee table?

There's a bowl of fruit on the coffee table.

1. What's on top of the TV?

_____

2. What's under the TV?

_____

3. What's between the man and the woman?

_____

4. What's outside of the window?

_____

5. What's next to the crayons?

_____

6. What's above the coffee table?

_____

7. Who's sleeping on the floor?

_____

8. What's next to the baby?

_____

9. What's behind the TV?

_____

10. What's beside the dog?

_____

Exercise 3.3. ***Using*** there is ***and*** there are. Look at the picture and write sentences using *there is* for singular subjects and *there are* for plural subjects. Use the correct preposition.

Examples: dog/floor *There is a dog on the floor.*

chairs/room *There are three chairs in the room.*

1. doll/baby _____

_____

2. picture of a bicycle/book _____

_____

3. man/chair _____

_____

4. TV/window _____

_____

5. two children/floor _____

_____

6. picture/coffee table _____

_____

7. drapes/window _____

_____

8. five people/room _____

_____

9. dog/ball _____

_____

10. tree/window _____

_____

EDITING YOUR OWN PARAGRAPH

Read your paragraph again. This time look for mistakes in grammar, punctuation, and spelling. Answer the questions on the chart below. Use the exercises that follow to help you make changes in your paragraph.

GRAMMAR, PUNCTUATION, SPELLING, FORMAT	YES	NO
Do you use *there is* and *there are* correctly?		
Are the prepositions (*to, on, above,* etc.) correct?		
Are the words spelled correctly?		
Is the paragraph indented?		
Is there a title?		
Is there a heading?		

◆ WRITING THE FINAL DRAFT

After you have edited, write the paragraph again in the correct format, as shown on page 6.

Using the Steps to Write about a Trip

◆ GETTING IDEAS

PLANNING A TRIP IN THE UNITED STATES

You have two weeks' vacation from school in December. Your friends have sent you post cards about some of the exciting places they have seen. What places would you like to visit? Look at the map and mark three states you want to see.

Greetings from Colorado

Rockport, Massachusetts

THE UNITED STATES

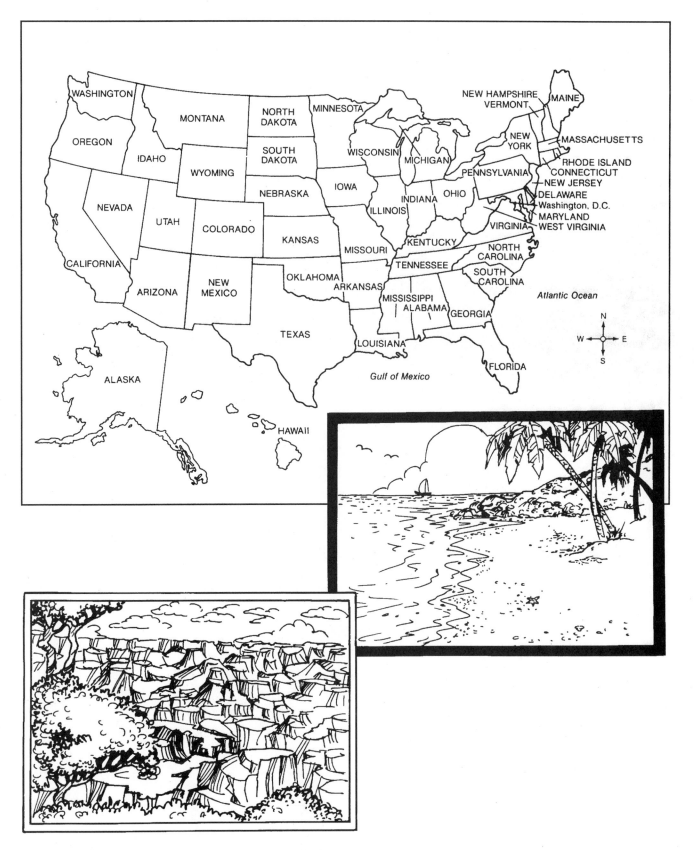

LISTING IDEAS

Complete the web that follows, or make a new one for your three places. Which state will you go to first? What will you see there? How long will you stay? Where will you go next? What do you want to see? What is the third place you will visit? What is important in this place?

FOCUSING, SUPPORTING, AND DRAFTING

Finish this composition about your trip. You have been given a main idea and some other words to begin sentences. Tell what you want to see in each place and how long you will stay.

There are three places in the United States that I want to visit. They are

_____, _____, and

_____. First, I want to go to _____

_____

_____

_____

Then, I want to visit _____

The last place I want to visit is _____

These are three special places in the United States that I always have wanted to see.

◆ REVISING

Exercise 3.4. *Following instructions to revise and edit.* Read this paragraph about Mexico City. Follow each instruction.

_____

Mexico City is my favorite place to visit it is an exciting city. Of course, I also enjoy Paris. I like to spend a day in the museum of anthropology. I also like visit the *zona rosa,* a place in the city where tourists can find many shops and restaurants. You can eat in Chinese restaurants, Japanese restaurants, Mexican restaurants, and Greek restaurants.

_____

_____

REVISING

1. Write a title for the paragraph.

2. Take out one sentence that does not fit with the others.

3. The last sentence repeats *restaurant* too many times. Make the sentence sound better by taking out the extra *restaurant* words.

4. Write a conclusion for the paragraph.

REVISING YOUR OWN COMPOSITION

Read your composition. Answer the questions on the chart after you read. Then make changes in the composition.

ORGANIZATION, IDEAS	YES	NO
Is there a main idea that tells three places you want to visit?		
Are there sentences that tell what you want to see in each place?		
Is there a final sentence that says the same idea as the first sentence?		

 EDITING

CAPITAL LETTERS FOR PLACES

Capitalize the names of geographic places: cities, states, countries, rivers, mountains, lakes, and special places (Statue of Liberty, Disneyland, Grand Canyon).

Exercise 3.5. Practicing capital letters for places. Add capital letters to names of places in these sentences.

    Example: I want to go river rafting on the $\overset{C}{c}$olorado $\overset{R}{r}$iver in the $\overset{G}{g}$rand $\overset{C}{c}$anyon.

1. disneyland is in anaheim, california.

2. I want to ski in the rocky mountains of colorado.

3. the grand canyon is in arizona.

4. florida has walt disney world and epcot center.

5. new york city is the largest city in the united states.

6. austin is the capital of texas.

7. lake tahoe is a beautiful place to visit.

8. rhode island is the smallest state in the u.s.

9. the mississippi river is the longest river in the u.s.

10. yellowstone national park is in wyoming.

VERB + TO + VERB

Some verbs have *to* after them if the next word is a verb.

    Example: I *want to visit* Disneyland.

Always use the simple form of the second verb. These are some verbs followed by *to:*

would like to	have to	hope to	plan to	expect to
forget to	like to	need to	want to	try to

Exercise 3.6. Using verb + to + verb. Use each verb in parentheses in a sentence. Underline the verb + *to* + verb in each sentence.

1. (expect) _____

_____

2. (forget) _____

_____

3. (have) _____

_____

4. (like) _____

_____

5. (need) _____

_____

6. (hope) _____

_____

7. (plan) _____

_____

8. (want) _____

_____

9. (try) _____

_____

10. (would like) _____

_____

Exercise 3.7. Finding mistakes. Now, find these four mistakes in the paragraph about Mexico City on page 57 and correct them.

1. The paragraph is not indented.

2. There is one sentence without a capital letter and a period.

3. Two names of places are not capitalized.

4. One verb is not correct. It needs to be changed to a verb + *to* + verb.

EDITING YOUR OWN COMPOSITION

Read your composition about the places you want to visit. Answer the questions on the chart and make the changes that you need.

GRAMMAR, PUNCTUATION, SPELLING, FORMAT	YES	NO
Are the verb tenses correct?		
Is there an infinitive *(to go, to visit)* after *want, plan, like*, etc.?		
Are there capital letters for place names?		
Are the words spelled correctly?		
Is the paragraph indented?		
Is there a title?		
Is there a heading?		

◆ WRITING THE FINAL DRAFT

Write your paragraph again in correct form.

Going the Extra Mile: Journal Writing

1. Write about a special place in your country. Why do tourists go there? What can they see? Draw a map that shows where the place is.

2. Plan a dream vacation to any place in the world. Where do you want to go? Why?

3. Write a letter to a friend who is planning to visit you. Tell about the places you want to take him or her.

Letay

Chapter 4

A BUSY LIFE: *Letay*

Do you sometimes feel there aren't enough hours in the day? Letay does. She is a student, a mother, and a worker. Letay goes to school two nights a week. She studies biology. Letay also works 30 hours a week. She does embroidery. Every day, when she is not working or studying, she cares for her son, Feleg. She plays with Feleg. She reads to him in English, and she talks to him in Tigrinya, her language in Ethiopia. Letay lives a busy life, but her husband, brother, and mother help her.

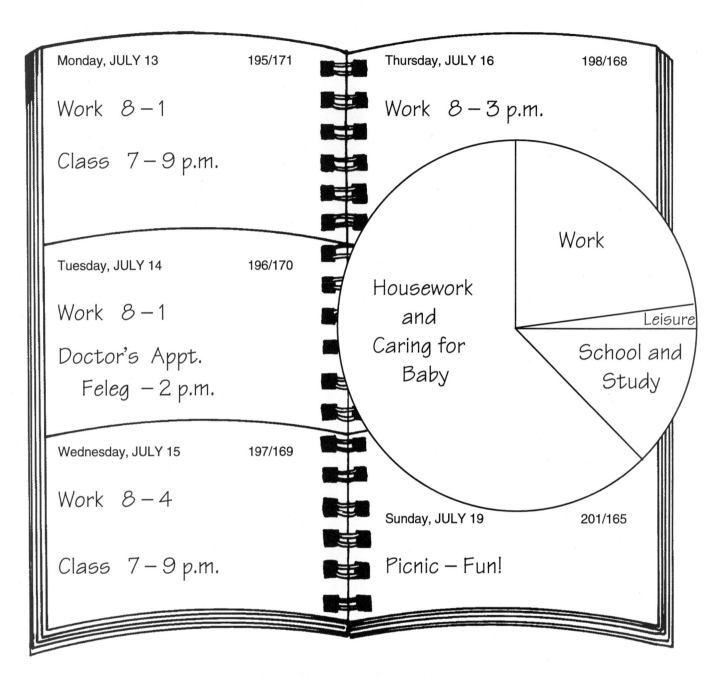

Chart of Letay's weekly activities

Using the Steps to Write about Weekly Activities

◆ GETTING IDEAS

Do you lead a busy life? What do you do each day? Each week? Look at the chart of Letay's weekly activities. Now fill in the circle with your weekly activities. Show your chart to a classmate. Explain what you do each week.

Chart of my weekly activities

◆ FOCUSING

Is your life busy? Is your life boring? Is your life fun? Finish this sentence:

I have a very _____ life. I am a student and a

_____ .

◆ SUPPORTING

You have just written your main idea. This is the first sentence of a paragraph about your life. What can you say to support the word that tells about your life? Look at the chart you have made. Add words to the chart that you may want to put in your paragraph.

DRAFTING

Now write your paragraph. Begin with the main idea sentence you wrote earlier.

My Life

I have a very _____ life. I am a student and a

_____. _____

_____

_____

_____

_____

_____

_____

_____

_____

_____

_____

_____

_____

_____

_____

I live a busy life, but _____.

 REVISING

THE PARTS OF A COMPOSITION

A good composition has a main idea sentence, supporting sentences, and a conclusion.

1. The **main idea sentence** is at the beginning and tells what the composition is about. In a paragraph, it is called a **topic sentence.** In a composition of several paragraphs, it is a **main idea.**

2. The **supporting sentences** give information to explain the main idea.

3. The **conclusion** is a sentence at the end that repeats the main idea in different words.

Exercise 4.1. Identifying the parts of a composition. Read the paragraph about Letay at the beginning of this chapter.

1. Circle the main idea sentence.

2. Underline the supporting sentences.

3. Underline the conclusion of the paragraph with two lines.

REVISING YOUR OWN PARAGRAPH

Read your own paper aloud. Then complete this checklist. Have you answered *no* to any questions? If so, make changes in your composition.

ORGANIZATION, IDEAS	YES	NO
Is there a main idea that says something about your life?		
Do all of the other sentences talk about this idea?		
Are there at least six sentences after the main idea that explain the parts of your life?		
Is there a final sentence that says the main idea again in different words?		

SIMPLE PRESENT TENSE

Rule: Use the simple present tense for habitual or repeated action (something you always or usually do). Also use it to give general information.

> **Examples:** I *drive* to school every day.
> He *likes* the computer class.
> She *wants* a job.
> Maria usually *drinks* coffee between classes.
> It *rains* a lot in April.
> You *study* from 6 to 9 P.M.
> We *play* soccer Saturday.
> They *watch* TV all the time.
> You two *work* harder than anyone else in the class.

Exercise 4.2. Choosing correct verbs. Study the examples above. Which subjects use the *-s* form of the verb?

_____   _____

_____   _____

Which subjects use the form of the verb with no *-s?*

_____   _____   _____

_____   _____

Put the correct form of the verb in the sentence. Be sure that subjects and verbs agree.

> **Example:** come   Sonya ___*comes*___ from Russia, but she
> live   ___*lives*___ in California now.

like   1. She _____ life in California.

stay   2. She _____ with her brother, Tola.

work   3. Tola and Sonya _____ 40 to 60 hours each week.

have   4. They do not _____ much time to cook dinner.

know   5. In fact, Tola does not _____ how to cook, and Sonya only _____ how to make spaghetti.

like   6. Tola _____ spaghetti, but he

miss   _____ the food from his own country.

call   7. Sonya _____ her mother in Russia once a month.

give   8. She _____ her many recipes for good food.

make   9. Now both Tola and Sonya _____ something other than spaghetti every night.

miss   10. Do you _____ a favorite food from your country?

EDITING YOUR OWN PARAGRAPH

Read your paragraph again. Answer these questions and edit any mistakes.

GRAMMAR, PUNCTUATION, SPELLING, FORMAT	YES	NO
Have you used the simple present tense correctly?		
Does every sentence begin with a capital letter and end with a period?		
Are the words spelled correctly?		
Is the paragraph indented?		
Is there a title?		
Is there a heading?		

◆ WRITING THE FINAL DRAFT

Write your paragraph again in correct form.

Using the Steps to Write about Another Culture

◆ GETTING IDEAS

GREETINGS IN OTHER COUNTRIES

Greetings are what we say and do when we meet other people. Greetings are an important part of each person's culture. For example, Americans are informal. They like to say *hi* or *hello* when they meet someone they know. *Nice to meet you* or *how do you do* are greetings Americans use when they meet someone for the first time. Sometimes Americans shake hands and sometimes they don't. When they don't see each other for a long time, close friends and family members often embrace or kiss.

How do people greet each other in another country? Talk to a student from a different country. Fill in the chart with information about his or her country.

NAME OF STUDENT _____ COUNTRY _____	
What do people *say* when they meet each other for the first time?	
What do people *do* when they meet for the first time? (bow? kiss? shake hands? etc.)	
What do you do and say when you meet a friend at school or work?	
Do you call friends by their first names when you greet them?	
Do you call teachers by their first names when you greet them?	
Do you call family members by first names?	
Do teenagers have any different greetings for each other?	
Are you formal or informal?	

Look at the information in the chart. Do you have other questions about greetings in your friend's country? What are the most interesting things you found out about greetings? Are these customs different from those in your country? Use the things you have found out for a paragraph about greeting in another country.

◆ DRAFTING

Greetings in _____

My classmate, _____, is from _____. She greets

people she meets very informally (formally). _____

_____

_____

_____

_____

_____

_____

_____

_____

_____

_____

_____

_____

_____

_____

 REVISING

Exercise 4.3. *Revising with a partner.* Read this paragraph. With a partner, answer the questions in the chart below. Then make changes to improve the paragraph and write it again.

> I am a very hard worker. In fact, I works twenty-four hours a day. My hands always move. I hang around the classroom, and the students and the teacher often look at my face. I am sometimes a little slow, sometimes a little fast, but they usually know that I will be right on time! Who or what am I?

ORGANIZATION, IDEAS	YES	NO
Is there a main idea sentence?		
Is there enough information for you to know what the paragraph is talking about?		
Is there any information that does not fit the main idea of "hard worker?"		

GRAMMAR, PUNCTUATION, SPELLING, FORMAT	YES	NO
Are there any mistakes in verbs?		
Are the words spelled correctly?		
Is there a title?		

REVISING YOUR OWN PARAGRAPH

Give your paragraph to the student who gave you information. Ask him or her to read your paragraph and to answer the questions on the following page. Use the answers to help you revise your paragraph.

ORGANIZATION, IDEAS	YES	NO
Does the main idea sentence say something about greetings in your country?		
Do all the other sentences give details of greetings?		
Is there a final sentence that repeats the main idea or compares greetings in the two countries?		
Is the information about your country correct?		

◆ EDITING

ADVERBS OF FREQUENCY

Adverbs of frequency tell how often something happens.

always	X	X	X	X	X	X	X	X	X	X
usually	X	X	X	X	X	X	X	X		
often	X	X	X	X	X	X	X			
sometimes	X	X	X	X						
rarely	X									
never										

Write adverbs of frequency **after** the verb *to be*.

It is *always* cold in January.
It is *usually* polite to say "good morning."

Write adverbs of frequency **before** other verbs.

It *always* rains in April.
I *sometimes* say "hi" to strangers who smile.

Exercise 4.4 Using adverbs of frequency. Fill in each blank with the adverb that tells how often you do these things. Use *always, usually, often, sometimes, rarely,* or *never.*

> **Example:** In my culture, I _____*usually*_____ shake hands when I meet a man.

1. I _____ bow when I meet an older person.

2. I _____ kiss my girlfriends on the cheek when I meet them at school.

3. It is _____ good to call your teachers by their last names.

4. In the U.S., I _____ call my teachers by their first names.

5. In my country, we _____ stand when the teacher comes into the room.

6. I _____ write letters to my parents.

7. I _____ telephone my mother and father.

8. Teenagers in the U.S. _____ give the "high five" greeting to each other.

9. People in my country are _____ formal in the way they greet each other.

10. I _____ hug my mother when I come back from a long trip.

EDITING YOUR OWN PARAGRAPH

Use what you have learned in the exercises to find mistakes in your own paragraph. Use the questions on the next page to help you. Make changes where necessary.

GRAMMAR, PUNCTUATION, SPELLING, FORMAT	YES	NO
Are there any mistakes in verb tenses?		
Are adverbs of frequency used correctly?		
Does each sentence begin with a capital letter and end with a period?		
Have you used a comma with *and* when it joins two complete sentences?		
Are words spelled correctly?		
Is the paragraph indented?		
Is there a title?		
Is there a heading?		

◆ WRITING THE FINAL DRAFT

Write your paragraph again. Make the changes that you have learned about in the exercises and on the charts.

Going the Extra Mile: Journal Writing

1. Compare the music that teenagers in your country like with music that American teens like.

2. Talk to an American about birthday parties in the U.S. What do Americans do at these parties? What do you do?

3. Compare shopping in two cities in the U.S. or compare shopping in your country and in the U.S.

Donna

Chapter 5

OUR ROOTS: *Donna*

The roots of a tree make it strong because they bring water and food from the soil to the tree. The tree's roots help it to stay straight in wind and rain. A human being's roots come from his or her culture. One generation passes them on to the next. These roots are important because they make us strong.

Donna's roots are Mexican and Aztec. The Aztecs lived in Mexico hundreds of years ago. Donna is proud of these roots. She has learned the dances of the Aztecs. Donna and other young Mexican-Americans make beautiful Aztec costumes. They wear these costumes when they dance at schools, festivals, and parties. Their dances teach others about the roots of the Mexican people.

Using the Steps to Write about Your Roots

◆ GETTING IDEAS

COMPLETING A WEB

What are your roots? What do you like best about your culture? What do you want to pass down to your children?

Write your ideas on the web. Try to be specific. For example, under *Language* you might write *Spanish* or under *Food* you might write names of dishes that are part of your family life.

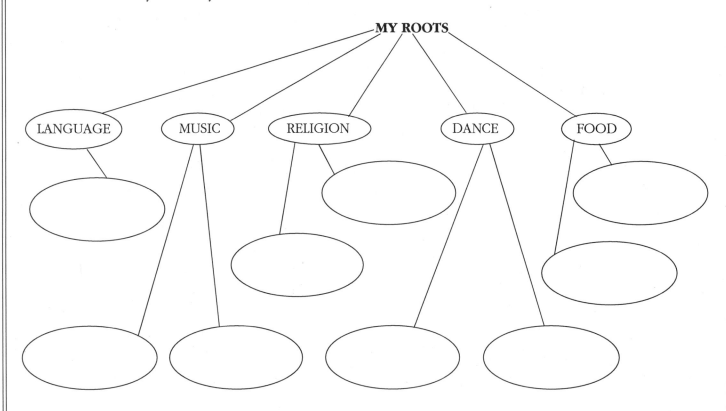

◆ FOCUSING

Look at your web. What three things do you like best about your culture? Write them below. Then make a sentence that has these three things.

1. _____

2. _____

3. _____

The three things I like best about my culture are _____

_____

_____.

◆ SUPPORTING AND DRAFTING

Use the sentence you wrote as the first sentence of your paragraph. Then write two or three sentences about each of the things you like most about your culture. End your paragraph with a sentence that says you want to pass these things down to your children.

My Roots

_____

_____

_____

_____

_____

_____

_____

_____

_____

_____

_____

_____

_____

_____

_____

_____

_____

REVISING A SAMPLE PARAGRAPH

Exercise 5.1. You be the teacher. Looking at another student's paragraph will help you to revise your own paragraph. Read Kyoung's composition. Answer the questions at the end of the paragraph. After you finish answering the questions, give Kyoung a grade for organization and ideas. If you answered *yes* to all the questions, give the composition an A (excellent). Give it a B (good) if you answered *yes* to most of the questions, and give it a C if you think the composition is satisfactory, but still needs some work. If you think there are a lot of problems, give it a D.

> Kyoung Lee
> May 10
> Writing I
>
> Two things I like best about Korean culture is respect for older people and love of education. First of all, I respect my mother and father. I listen to my mother and father. I never talk bad to them. I always polite. Because I respect them. Education is also important. A man is nothing without education.

ORGANIZATION, IDEAS	YES	NO
Is there a main idea that tells which things Kyoung likes about his culture?		
Does he write several sentences about each thing?		
Do these sentences help you to understand the specific things?		
Does the last sentence say he wants to pass these on to his children?		
Does Kyoung choose words that are clear and help you to understand?		

What grade on organization would you give Kyoung? _____

REVISING YOUR OWN PARAGRAPH

Answer the same questions about your own paragraph. Give yourself a grade on organization and ideas.

ORGANIZATION, IDEAS	YES	NO
Is there a main idea that tells some things you like about your culture?		
Do you write several sentences about each thing?		
Do these sentences help the reader to understand the things you like?		
Does the last sentence say that you want to pass these on to your children?		
Do you choose words that are clear and help the reader to understand?		

What grade on organization would you give yourself? _____

◆ EDITING

EDITING A SAMPLE PARAGRAPH

Exercise 5.2. Editing another student's paragraph. Now read Kyoung's paragraph for mistakes in grammar, punctuation, spelling, and format.

GRAMMAR, PUNCTUATION, SPELLING, FORMAT	YES	NO
Are there any mistakes in verb tenses?		
Is there a period at the end of each sentence?		
Are the words spelled correctly?		
Is the paragraph indented?		
Is there a title?		
Is there a heading? (name, date, class)		

What grade on grammar, punctuation, and spelling would you give Kyoung? _____

EDITING YOUR OWN PARAGRAPH

Read your paragraph again and mark the chart. Give yourself a grade.

GRAMMAR, PUNCTUATION, SPELLING, FORMAT	YES	NO
Are there any mistakes in verb tenses?		
Is there a period at the end of each sentence?		
Are the words spelled correctly?		
Is the paragraph indented?		
Is there a title?		
Is there a heading? (name, date, class)?		

What grade on grammar, punctuation, and spelling would you give yourself? _____

♦ WRITING THE FINAL DRAFT

Write your paragraph again. Use what you have learned in the revision and editing exercises to improve your paragraph.

Using the Steps to Write about a Family

♦ GETTING IDEAS

TALKING ABOUT A FAMILY TREE

Study the Martínez family tree. Choose one person in the Martínez family. What can you tell the class about that person?

THE MARTINEZ FAMILY

María
45 years old
Mexico City

José
56 years old
Mexico City

Rita
21 years old
Reno, Nevada

Manuel
26 years old
Reno, Nevada

Gloria
23 years old
Dallas, Texas

Donna
24 years old
Los Angeles,
California

John
28 years old
Los Angeles,
California

Susie
2 years old
Reno, Nevada

John Jr.
2 years old
Los Angeles, California

Example: Susie is two years old. She is the daughter of Rita and Manuel. She lives in Reno, Nevada. Her grandparents live in Mexico City.

Family Words

mother	sister	husband	cousin
father	brother	wife	grandmother
daughter	uncle	niece	grandfather
son	aunt	nephew	grandson

◆ FOCUSING

You have been talking about each person in the Martínez family. Now what can you say about the whole family? Answer these questions with complete sentences.

1. Is the Martínez family a large family? a medium-sized family? a small family?

_____

_____

2. Where do all the members of the Martínez family live?

_____

_____

3. Can you think of other important things you might say about the Martínez family?

_____

_____

_____

◆ SUPPORTING

Use an idea about the Martínez family from the sentences you just wrote. This will be the main idea of your paragraph. How can you support this idea? Look at the Martínez family tree for facts that support your main idea.

◆ DRAFTING

Write a paragraph about the Martínez family. Use all you have learned in other chapters to make it a good paragraph.

_____

_____

_____

_____

_____

_____

_____

_____

_____

_____

_____

_____

_____

_____

◆ REVISING

WRITING CONCLUSIONS

In a short composition, a conclusion is a sentence that summarizes everything that has been written.

The conclusion   1) can say again the idea in the topic or main idea sentence,
               2) can ask a question,
               3) can make an exclamation (a strong statement!).

Exercise 5.3. Finding main ideas and conclusions. In the paragraph that follows, underline the main idea once and the conclusion twice.

My First Day on the Job

      My first day of work at Fast Burger was one of the worst days of my life. First of all, I burned my hand when I was cooking French fries. I tried to put a Band-Aid on my hand, but I dropped it into the hot oil. Before I could say "Stop!" another worker had served the Band-Aid and the fries to a customer. The customer got mad. My manager got mad, and I almost got fired. What an awful day this was!

What kind of conclusion was it? _____

Now write two different conclusions for the paragraph.

1. A question: _____

_____

2. A statement: _____

_____

REVISING YOUR PARAGRAPH

Use the chart that follows to check your paragraph about the Martínez family. If you answer *no* to any of the questions, make changes in your paragraph.

ORGANIZATION, IDEAS	YES	NO
Is there a main idea that says something general about the family?		
Do the other sentences support the main idea?		
Is there a last sentence that ties up the other ideas?		
Are the family words used correctly?		

◆ EDITING

MAKING NOUNS POSSESSIVE

Add *'s* to make the singular possessive.

Write this.   *Do not write this.*

María's daughter   the daughter of María

Rita's husband   the husband of María

Exercise 5.4. Showing possession. Look at the Martínez family tree and read these sentences about the family. Fill in each space with one word.

1. María is _____ wife.

2. José is _____ husband.

3. Rita is _____ sister. She is also _____ sister.

4. Susie is María's and _____ granddaughter.

5. Susie is _____ cousin.

6. Donna is _____ wife.

7. Manuel is _____ husband.

8. Donna is _____ aunt.

9. John is _____ uncle.

10. Gloria is _____ aunt. She is also _____ aunt.

MAKING THE PLURAL OF FAMILY NOUNS

Add *s* to form the plural of nouns. one sister three sisters one cousin two cousins one brother four brothers	Some plurals are irregular. Do not add *s*. one child six children one man two men one woman three women

Exercise 5.5. Plurals of family nouns. Fill in each blank with the correct singular or plural noun. Use the Martínez family tree.

1. Donna and John have one _____.

2. María and José have three _____. They are all daughters.

3. Rita and Gloria are _____.

4. Susie and John Jr. are _____.

5. José, Manuel, and John are _____.

6. María, Rita, Gloria, and Donna are the _____ of the Martínez

   family.

7. Susie and John Jr. are little _____.

8. Rita and Manuel only have one _____.

Exercise 5.6. Editing for plurals and singulars. Eleven plural or singular nouns are italicized. Some are correct and some are not. Check each one and change the ones that are not correct.

My Grandmother

My grandmother is a very important part of my family. She is 85 *years* old, but she still works hard and remembers everything about her family. She had eight *childs*. Two of them were *son* and six were *daughters*. My grandmother was only 15 *year* old when she got married and 35 when she had her last *child*. This was a very big family for a young *women*. Now my grandmother has 25 *grandchilds*. Ten of them are *girl* and 15 are *boys*. What a big *families*!

EDITING YOUR OWN PARAGRAPH

Read your paragraph about the Martínez family. Then check it against the chart that follows. Make changes.

GRAMMAR, PUNCTUATION, SPELLING, FORMAT	YES	NO
Are the verbs correct?		
Are the possessives correct?		
Are the plurals correct?		
Is there a period at the end of each sentence?		
Are the words spelled correctly?		
Is the paragraph indented?		
Is there a title?		
Is there a heading (name, class, date)?		

◆ WRITING THE FINAL DRAFT

Use what you have learned in the revision and editing exercises to write your final draft.

Going the Extra Mile: Journal Writing

1. Do you have a favorite family member? Write about him or her.

2. Is there something you own—a piece of jewelry, a book, a photo—that you would want to give to your son or daughter? What is it? Why is it important?

3. Do you look or act like someone else in your family? Who? How are you alike?

Elli

Chapter 6

COOKING AND EATING: *Elli*

Elli learned to cook when she was a girl in Cyprus. Now, she likes to prepare Cypriot food for her family, and they love to eat the food she serves them. She often invites relatives and friends to join them, too. This is what they say when they have dinner.

"Please, Sophia, have some more meat," Elli says.

"Well, just a little. Everything is so delicious."

"Pete, would you like some macaroni?" she asks.

"Sure, I'd love some, and may I have a little more salad, please?"

"Of course, of course. Stella, please pass the salad to him. Now, who wants dessert? There's some lovely baklava."

Sophia answers, "Oh, it sounds great, but I just can't eat anything else!"

"Well, how about some fruit? Would you like some grapes or a piece of melon?"

"O.K., thanks. I'll have just a few grapes."

"Would anyone like a cup of coffee?" asks Elli.

"Yes, please. This is a wonderful meal!" they all say.

Elli just smiles. It makes her happy when her family and friends enjoy the food she prepares.

Using the Steps to Write about Eating Customs

◆ GETTING IDEAS

INTERVIEWING A CLASSMATE

Ask your partner these questions about lunch or dinner in his or her country. Ask some questions of your own, too.

What time do you usually eat? _____

Where do you eat? (kitchen, dining room, living room?)

_____

Where do you sit? (on the floor, at a table?)

_____

Who usually eats with you? _____

What do you do while you are eating? _____

How do you eat? (with chopsticks, a fork, your hands?)

_____

What are some typical kinds of food that you eat?

_____

Now, make a short list of the same information about the same meal in your country.

Time: _____

Place: _____

People: _____

Activities: _____

Utensils: _____

Food: _____

_____

◆ FOCUSING

Are your friend's eating customs the same as yours or different from yours? Complete this sentence.

Eating customs in _____ are _____

_____ eating customs in my country.

◆ SUPPORTING AND DRAFTING

COMPARING EATING CUSTOMS

Begin your first draft with the sentence you just wrote. Use the information your friend gave you to write about meals in his country. Then, indent and make a new paragraph to write about meals in your country.

_____

Eating customs in _____ are _____

_____ eating customs in my country. For example, in

_____ they _____

_____

_____

_____

_____

_____

_____

_____

In my country, _____, we _____

_____

_____

_____

_____

_____

_____

◆ REVISING

When you write a longer composition that talks about more than one thing, you should divide it into paragraphs. Each time you begin to write about a new idea, you need to indent to start a new paragraph.

Exercise 6.1. Identifying paragraphs. Read the following composition. Find the place where the second paragraph should begin. Then, write a main idea sentence that tells what the whole composition is about. Give the composition a title.

Here in the United States, my daughters and I usually do our grocery shopping at a huge supermarket. First, we make a long list of all the things that we need for a whole week. Then, on Saturday morning, we take the car and drive to Super Saver. We spend more than an hour filling the shopping cart with everything from artichokes to toothpaste. We usually have to stand in line for a long time at the checkout counter. Finally, we load everything in the car, drive home, and put all of the groceries away. When we are finished, we are usually very tired. At home in Guatemala, we sometimes go to a supermarket, but we also have small grocery stores in every neighborhood. We can walk from our house to the store, and we just pick out the fruit, vegetables, and other things we need for a day or two. We usually stop to chat for a few minutes with neighbors and with the shopkeeper. If we get home and see that we forgot something, we just send one of the children back to the store to get it. American supermarkets are very nice, but I sometimes miss our small neighborhood store.

♦ REVISING YOUR COMPOSITION

Use this chart to check your composition about eating habits in your friend's country and in your country. Make any necessary changes.

ORGANIZATION, IDEAS	YES	NO
Is there a main idea sentence?		
Are there at least six sentences about eating customs in your partner's country?		
Is there a second paragraph about eating in your country?		
Is there a conclusion that tells how your customs are the same or different?		

♦ EDITING

COMBINING SENTENCES WITH *BUT*

But connects two ideas that are different.

Exercise 6.2. Conjunctions. Read this story and underline the conjunction *but*.

The Problem with English

I am new in this country, and my English is new, too. Sometimes I don't say words correctly. One day I went to the supermarket to get something easy to fix for dinner. I like chicken soup, and I was looking for a can of this good food. I saw tomato, bean, and vegetable soup, but I didn't see chicken.

A nice girl asked me, "Can I help you find something?"

"Thank you," I said. "I want some kitchen soap."

"Kitchen soap?" she asked. "You're in the wrong place, but I can help you."

I followed her to a place that had many things to clean the house. She handed me a big bottle of green liquid, and then she told me to have a nice day. I smiled and thanked her. She was pretty, helpful, and nice. I took the green soap, and then I went home. I was still hungry, but I had met a new friend.

How do we punctuate sentences with *but?*

96

Exercise 6.3. *Completing sentences* with *but*. Add a logical ending to each of these sentences.

1. In my country we eat a lot of fresh fruit, but here we

   _____.

2. Here I usually buy bread from the supermarket, but back home my mother

   _____.

3. My roommate likes to drink frozen juice, but I

   _____.

4. In my country, most people go home for lunch at noon, but in the United

   States they

   _____.

5. I know that Coke and chocolate are not very nutritious, but

   _____.

6. Americans like to eat a lot of fast food, but

   _____.

7. Americans often eat dinner around six o'clock, but my family

   _____.

8. I don't know how to cook very well, but I sometimes

   _____.

9. We usually eat a lot of vegetables and rice, but we don't eat

   _____.

10. In this country, you can order some kinds of food by telephone, but

   _____.

USING COMMAS FOR ITEMS IN A SERIES

When we list only two things, we use *and* without a comma.

Example: I usually drink my coffee with milk and sugar.

When we list three or more things, we use a comma after each thing.

Example: We need to buy coffee, eggs, and bread.

Exercise 6.4. Adding commas. Put commas in the sentences with lists of three or more things.

1. For breakfast, we usually have coffee juice and cereal.

2. My father likes to eat ham and eggs, but I don't.

3. Mangoes papayas pineapples and bananas are popular kinds of fruit in my country.

4. In our school cafeteria, they serve hamburgers sandwiches soup and salad.

5. Are there any apples and oranges in the basket?

6. To make this cake, you need flour sugar eggs and oil.

EDITING YOUR COMPOSITION

Now use this chart to help you correct your composition about eating customs in your country and in your partner's country.

GRAMMAR, PUNCTUATION, SPELLING, FORMAT	YES	NO
Are the conjunctions *but* and *and* correct?		
Are all the verbs correct?		
Is there a period at the end of every sentence?		
Does every sentence begin with a capital letter?		
Are the paragraphs indented?		
Is your spelling correct?		

♦ WRITING THE FINAL DRAFT

After you have made changes, write your composition again.

Using the Steps to Write a Recipe

♦ GETTING IDEAS

PLANNING A CLASS DINNER

Decide who will bring the soup, the salad, the main dishes, the dessert, and the drinks. Each person should write a recipe for the thing he or she plans to make.

What is a popular food or drink in your country? Can you explain to the class how to make it? Make a list of the things you need and a list of the main things you have to do.

_____
(name of food or drink)

Ingredients:

_____   _____

_____   _____

_____   _____

_____

Steps:

_____

_____

_____

_____

_____

◆ FOCUSING

Now write a main idea sentence that tells the name of the food you are going to make and something about it.

_____

◆ SUPPORTING AND DRAFTING

Check your list to be sure you have all the important steps and ingredients. Then write your first draft. Begin with your main idea sentence. Put your steps and ingredients into sentences. Use correct paragraph form.

_____

_____

_____

_____

_____

_____

_____

_____

_____

_____

_____

◆ REVISING

When you write a recipe, it is important to give exact amounts for the ingredients. Also, it is necessary to put the steps in the correct order.

Exercise 6.5. Revising a recipe. Read this recipe for lemonade. Answer the following questions. Make the necessary changes.

> Add a little sugar and mix the sugar and lemon juice. Squeeze some lemons in a large pitcher. Put in about one liter of cold water. Stir the mixture. Add a few ice cubes, and pour the lemonade into tall glasses. If you like, you can put a sprig of fresh mint in each glass. Fresh lemonade is a great drink for a hot summer day.

1. Does the paragraph have a title?
2. Is there a main idea sentence that tells what you are making?
3. Are the steps in the correct order?
4. Does the recipe tell how many lemons and how much sugar you need?

REVISING YOUR COMPOSITION

Now use the questions in the chart below to help you make changes in your own recipe.

ORGANIZATION, IDEAS	YES	NO
Does the paragraph have a title?		
Is there a main idea sentence that tells what you are making?		
Are the steps in the correct order?		
Do you have specific amounts for all of the ingredients?		
Are the steps clear and easy to understand?		
Do you have some connecting words like *first, then, next?*		
Is there a conclusion that repeats the name of what you are making?		

USING COUNT AND NONCOUNT NOUNS

We can count some nouns such as *carrot, apple, cookie*. Count nouns can be singular (one) or plural (more than one): *banana, bananas*

We do not count other nouns such as *tea, juice, bread*. Noncount nouns have no plural form. When we want to tell how much or many, we put some words before the nouns.

SINGULAR	PLURAL	NONCOUNT
a, an	some	some
a potato	some potatoes	some milk
one	two, three (any number)	
one peach	three peaches	
	a few	a little
	a few lemons	a little tea
	a can of peas	a can of soup
	two kilos of bananas	four pounds of beef

Exercise 6.6. Listing count and noncount nouns.   How is your nutrition? Do you eat a healthful diet, or can you do better? Write down what you ate and drank yesterday. List everything. Give amounts.

Examples: five bottles of soda   an orange

_____   _____

_____   _____

_____   _____

_____   _____

_____   _____

Give yourself a score on what you ate.

**** Very healthful   ** Need to go grocery shopping

*** Good, but not perfect   * Junk food junkie

USING THE IMPERATIVE

When we give directions or instructions, we can use the simple form of the verb without any ending. We do not need a subject in the sentence.

Examples: Please close the door.
Fill the pot with warm water.
Turn left on Santa Fe Drive and go south for two miles.

Exercise 6.7. Writing imperative sentences. Poor Uncle Ricardo! He wants to make a cup of tea, but he can't remember how. Can you help him? Use the words given to make good sentences for each picture.

1. fill/kettle/water

_____

_____

2. put/kettle/stove

_____

_____

3. turn on/stove

_____

_____

4. let/water/boil

_____

_____

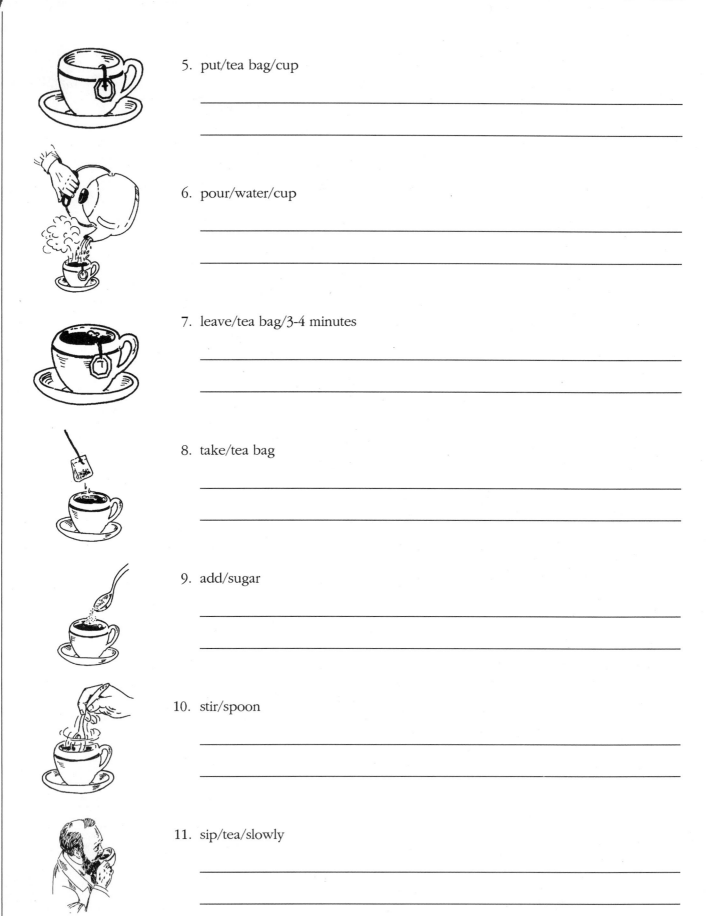

5. put/tea bag/cup

_____

_____

6. pour/water/cup

_____

_____

7. leave/tea bag/3-4 minutes

_____

_____

8. take/tea bag

_____

_____

9. add/sugar

_____

_____

10. stir/spoon

_____

_____

11. sip/tea/slowly

_____

_____

EDITING YOUR COMPOSITION

Answer these questions about your own recipe on page 100. If you answer *no* to any questions, correct those errors.

GRAMMAR, PUNCTUATION, SPELLING, FORMAT	YES	NO
Are the imperative verbs correct?		
Did you use count and noncount nouns correctly?		
Does every sentence have a capital letter and a period?		
Did you use commas between items in a list?		
Is your spelling correct?		

◆ WRITING THE FINAL DRAFT

After you finish revising and editing your composition, write it again on another piece of paper.

Going the Extra Mile: Journal Writing

1. Describe your favorite fast food restaurant. What kinds of food do they serve? What does the restaurant look like? Why do you like to eat there?

2. Tell about a typical breakfast with your family. What do you eat? What time do you have breakfast? Who eats with you?

3. Describe the most unusual food you have ever eaten. Where were you? What did you eat? Why did you think it was strange? How did you feel?

Tran

Chapter 7

A LIFE BEYOND THAT: *TRAN*

I have a new life now, but for many years it was a sad life. Nine years ago, I left Vietnam. My father took me in the middle of the night. He didn't want my mother to worry. I left my home forever. I never said good-bye to my mother, my sisters, or my brothers. My father and I went to camps in Thailand and then the Philippines.

Finally, an American family helped us and we came to the United States. I was happy because I went to Lincoln High School in Denver, Colorado. I lived in a small apartment with a friend. I slept and studied in the closet of my friend's bedroom. I cleaned rooms and halls at the school for $4.85 an hour. After work I had nothing to do, so I played the piano in the music room. It was really fun! I liked this music so much that I took classes and also learned guitar and singing.

This year I graduated from Lincoln High School and I am going to college soon. If I don't keep studying, I'll work forever at $5 an hour. I want a life beyond that.

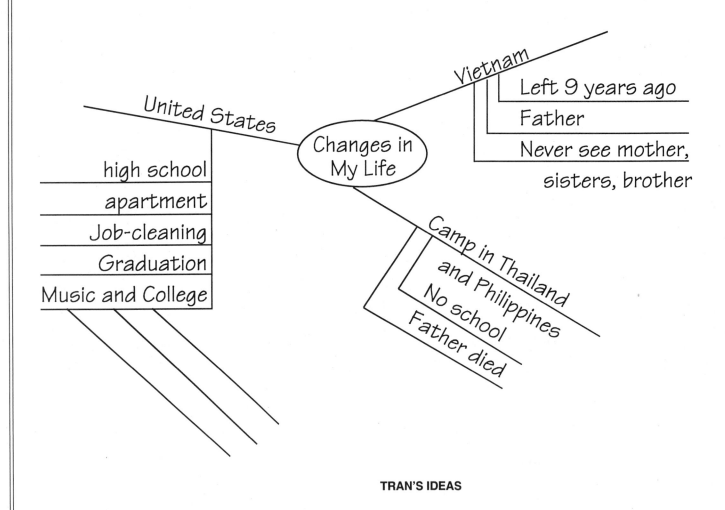

TRAN'S IDEAS

Exercise 7.1. What steps did Tran follow?

1. Tran put his ideas on the *map* above. He wrote down some words that tell about Vietnam and about the United States, but he didn't finish the map with ideas about music and college. Add three ideas about Tran's music and his college plans.

2. What three parts does Tran have in his composition?

A. _____

B. _____

C. _____

3. What is the main idea of Tran's composition? Write down the sentence that says his main idea.

_____

_____

4. There are two ideas on Tran's map that he did not use in his composition. Find these ideas and cross them out on the map.

5. Most of the verbs in Tran's composition were in the past tense. Read the composition again and underline all the past tense verbs. Then complete the chart that follows by writing in the simple past tense of each present tense verb.

SIMPLE PRESENT	PAST
is	
leave	
take	
doesn't	
says	
go	
help	
come	
live	

SIMPLE PRESENT	PAST
sleep	
study	
clean	
have	
play	
like	
learn	
graduate	

Using the Steps to Tell about Your Past

◆ GETTING IDEAS

MAKING A MAP

Can you think of a time from your past life that you would like to write about? An exciting time? An important time? A happy or sad time?

On the map below, write your ideas. Put general ideas on long lines and details on short lines.

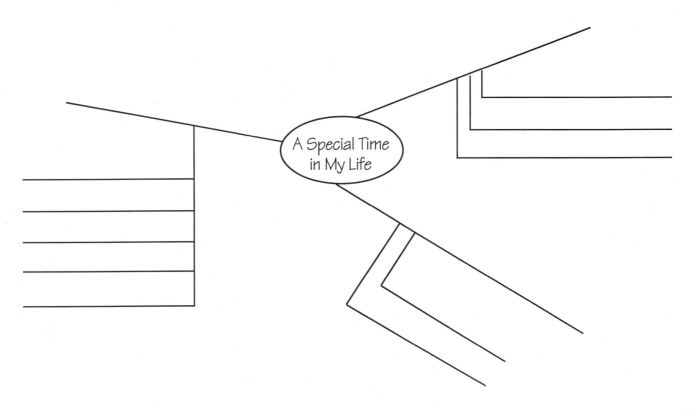

A Special Time in My Life

◆ FOCUSING

Look at your map of ideas. What is the main idea? What do you think about this time in your life?

_____ was _____
      (time in life)   (what do you think about it?)

Examples: My trip to England was exciting.
My first ski trip was frightening.
High school was the most important time in my life.

◆ SUPPORTING

Look back at your map. Are there ideas you can use to support your main idea? Circle them. Are there ideas that don't fit your main idea. Cross them out. Are there ideas you want to add to the map?

◆ DRAFTING

Write the main idea. Follow it with details from your map. Think of a conclusion that ties together the ideas and says again what you wrote in your main idea. Try to write at least two paragraphs in your composition.

_____

_____

_____

_____

_____

_____

_____

_____

_____

_____

_____

_____

_____

_____

_____

_____

_____

TELLING A STORY

A story does not always begin with a main idea. Sometimes that idea comes close to the end of the story because it builds suspense. In other words, it makes the reader want to find out what is going to happen.

Exercise 7.2. *Writing the ending of a story.* Read the beginning of a story below. Finish the composition with at least eight sentences. Write a title for it. Then share your story with the class.

_____

It was a black, rainy night. John had just finished his 8 o'clock class at the college. He got wet as he ran from the classroom building to his old car. Then he drove two miles to his apartment. As he parked his car, he looked up at the windows of his apartment.

"That's strange," he thought. "There's a green light coming from my bedroom window. What is it? Nobody but me has a key to the apartment."

John's heart was beating loudly as he slowly walked up the stairs to the door of his apartment. He put the key in the keyhole and turned it carefully. When he opened the door, _____

_____

_____

_____

_____

_____

_____

_____

_____

REVISING YOUR OWN PARAGRAPH

Read the first draft of your composition about a past time in your life. Answer the questions on the chart. Make changes if you need to.

ORGANIZATION, IDEAS	YES	NO
Is there a main idea sentence that tells about a past time in your life?		
Do all of the other sentences tell something about this time?		
Are there enough sentences to make your reader understand why this time was important to you?		
Is there a sentence at the end that says your main idea again?		

♦ EDITING

PAST TENSE OF REGULAR VERBS

Use the *-ed* ending to form the past tense of regular verbs in the affirmative only. Do not use the *-ed* ending with verbs in the question and negative forms.

> **Examples: Affirmative**
> We *washed* the clothes yesterday.
> I *worked* hard all week.
> Tran *waited* a long time to come to America.

Use *did* to make questions and *did not* to make negatives.

> **Examples:**
>
> **Question**
> *Did* you *work* hard all week?
> *Did* you *call* me today?
>
> **Negative**
> I *didn't work* hard.
> I *didn't call* you.

Exercise 7.3. Recognizing regular verbs. Read the composition you just wrote. What regular verbs did you use? Write each regular verb below.

_____   _____

_____   _____

_____   _____

_____   _____

IRREGULAR VERBS

An irregular past tense verb does not end in *-ed*. There are many irregular verb forms in the past tense. Use them in the affirmative only.

Here are a few irregular verbs.

PRESENT TENSE	PAST TENSE	EXAMPLE
leave	left	I *left* my country in 1990.
is	was	It *was* a sad time.
buy	bought	I *bought* an old car.
go	went	I *went* to high school.

Exercise 7.4. *Recognizing irregular verbs.* Read the composition you just wrote. Did you use any irregular verbs? Write them below.

_____   _____

_____   _____

_____   _____

Exercise 7.5. *Using regular and irregular verbs.* Finish this story by putting the present tense verbs into the past tense. If you don't know the correct form, check the chart of irregular verbs in the Appendix on page 147.

An Awful Birthday Party

When I _____ (am) ten years old, my sister _____ (has) a birthday party for me. She _____ (asks) six of my friends to the party. She also _____ (asks) Kim, but my sister _____ (does) not know that I _____ (do) not like Kim.

At the party, we _____ (play) some games, but Kim _____ (wins) every game. "I'm smarter than you are," Kim _____ (says) to me. I _____ (get) angry with Kim.

Then it _____ (is) time to eat. There _____ (is) a beautiful chocolate cake on the table. It _____ (has) eight candles on it. "Blow the candles out," my sister _____ (says). I _____ (take) a deep breath and before I _____ (blow), Kim _____ (pulls) the cake in front of her on the table. Now I _____ (become) really angry. I _____ (move) the cake back to my place, but I _____ (pull) too hard. The cake _____ (falls) on the floor. What a mess! And what an awful birthday.

EDITING YOUR OWN COMPOSITION

Read the first draft of your composition on page 111 about a past time in your life. Answer the questions on the chart. Make changes.

GRAMMAR, PUNCTUATION, SPELLING, FORMAT	YES	NO
Do you use the correct forms of the past tense?		
Does every sentence start with a capital letter and end with a period, question mark, or exclamation point?		
Are the words spelled correctly?		
Is the paragraph indented?		
Is there a heading (name, class, date)?		
Is there a title?		

◆ WRITING THE FINAL DRAFT

Use what you have learned in the revising and editing exercises. Write your composition again.

Using the Steps to Write about Life in the Past

♦ GETTING IDEAS

Do you know someone in their seventies or eighties? You can find out many interesting things about the past by asking questions of an elderly person. Think of an older friend or relative. What questions would you ask them about life when they were children?

Here is part of a tape recording that a student made. She asked many questions about the past. Read the answers he gave her. Think about how you would write these answers into a composition of at least three paragraphs.

TRANSCRIPT OF INTERVIEW

What's your name? Walter Floyd Shoemaker

When were you born? I was born in 1908 in Lynn County, Kansas.

Where did you live when you were a child? I lived on a farm in Kansas until I was ten years old. Then I moved to Colorado.

How many children were there in your family? I had three sisters.

Did you work on the farm? I worked from the time I was old enough to walk. I fed the chickens, gathered eggs, helped in the fields, milked cows, branded cattle, and did anything my father needed me to do. I remember helping my father butcher a sheep when I was only five years old.

Did you go to school? Oh, yes, of course. I started school when I was six, but I had to get up about 4:30 a.m. to help with the cows. Then we had a big breakfast with eggs, bacon, potatoes, bread, just like a dinner. After breakfast, I walked about an hour to school. Once in a while my Dad would let me and my sisters take one or two of the horses and we all rode to school.

Was it a big school? Oh my, no. It just had two rooms. The little kids were in one room and the kids over ten years old in another room. There were just 18 kids in the school.

What did you wear to school? When it was warm, we wore overalls and a shirt. My family didn't have much money, so many times, I had to wear shoes that came from my sisters. I remember how happy I was when I got my first new pair of shoes. It was on my tenth birthday.

Your life sounds very hard. Did you have any fun? Oh, yes, we had fun. We played ball at school and fished and hunted ducks and deer. Because my family had Cherokee Indian blood, we also made Indian headdresses and learned a lot about Indian life.

◆ FOCUSING

What do you think about life in the United States 75 years ago? Was it an exciting life? A difficult life? A simple life? What about life in other places 75 years ago? What was it like? Your answer to these questions is your main idea. Write it here:

Life in _____ years ago was

_____.

◆ SUPPORTING

USING AN INTERVIEW

Now look back at the answers to the questions in the transcript, or interview an older person you know. Which answers are most interesting? Which ones best support your main idea? Put a check mark beside these. Cross out any ideas you don't want to use.

◆ DRAFTING

Use your main idea as the first sentence. Then tell the name and age of the person who gave you the information. Follow this with Mr. Shoemaker's ideas about his life as a child.

_____

_____

_____

_____

_____

_____

_____

_____

_____

_____

PARTS OF A GOOD PARAGRAPH

A good paragraph begins with a **topic sentence.** A topic sentence is a general idea. Then a good paragraph adds **supporting details,** which are more specific. It ends with a **conclusion** that says the topic sentence in different words.

**Topic
Sentence**

1. _____

2. __D_____

3. __F_____

**Supporting
Sentences**

4. _____

5. _____

6. _____

7. _____

8. _____

9. _____

10. _____

Conclusion

11. ____

Exercise 7.6. Organizing sentences in a paragraph.   Read the sentences that follow. Organize them so they make a good paragraph. Write the letters of each sentence in order on the diagram above. The second and third sentences have been done for you.

A. The careless driver was a woman.

B. A bad event in my life last year turned into something good.

C. She was busy talking to a friend and didn't see the red light.

D. The bad thing was that a driver ran into the back of my car when I stopped for a red light.

E. My car is still a mess, but I have a great girl friend.

F. After the crash, I jumped out of the car.

G. We started dating.

H. She was beautiful, with long black hair and green eyes!

I. The careless driver was a woman.

J. I was really mad!

K. Then I met the driver.

REVISING YOUR OWN PARAGRAPH

Read your composition and answer these questions about it. Use your answers to make any changes that are necessary.

ORGANIZATION, IDEAS	YES	NO
Is there a main idea sentence that says something about life 75 years ago?		
Do all of the other sentences tell something specific about this time?		
Are there at least ten sentences that give details about life at this time?		
Is there a sentence at the end that repeats the main idea in other words?		

CHOOSING VERB TENSES

Most of your composition will be in simple past tense, but you will also need to use the simple present when you give facts about Mr. Shoemaker today.

REVIEW OF TENSES

Simple present   Makes a statement of fact or tells what usually happens
Now I *live* in Littleton, Colorado.

Simple past   Describes an action that is finished
In 1908, I *lived* in Kansas. I *worked* hard then.

Exercise 7.7. Choosing present or past tense.   Each verb is italicized in the paragraph that follows. Decide if the verb should be in the simple present or simple past tense. There are eight mistakes. Correct them.

My Grandmother

Today my grandmother *is* 80 years old, but she still *remembered* the hard life she *had* when she *was* younger. Her father *dies* when she *was* only 10 years old. She *took* care of her five brothers and sisters because her mother *was* sick with tuberculosis. She *made* soap, *washed* all the clothes, *cook* the meals, *clean* the house, and *grew* vegetables for the family. Her mother *died* when she *was* 15 years old, and she *marries* my grandfather when she *is* 18. My grandparents *have* five children of their own, and my grandmother *worked* hard for this large family, too. Today she *remembers* the hard work, but she also *remembered* the good times with her family.

EDITING YOUR OWN COMPOSITION

Read your composition again. Answer the questions below and make necessary changes.

GRAMMAR, PUNCTUATION, SPELLING, FORMAT	YES	NO
Do you use present and past tense correctly?		
Does every sentence begin with a capital letter and end with a period, question mark, or exclamation point?		
Are words spelled correctly?		
Are the paragraphs indented?		
Is there a title?		
Is there a heading?		

♦ WRITING THE FINAL DRAFT

Use what you have learned in the revision and editing exercises to write your composition a final time.

Going the Extra Mile: Journal Writing

1. Interview an older person whom you know. Write about life when he or she was a child.

2. Write about a special birthday or holiday when you were a child.

3. Write about your first day in elementary or high school. Was it an exciting day? A terrible day?

Bai

Chapter 8

A PLACE IN THE FUTURE: *BAI*

Bai comes from Beijing, China. She and her husband are studying in the United States now. Both of them work very hard because they know that a good education will be important for their futures.

Bai writes: "I plan to study for an American master's degree after I finish my English school. Because I have already got a bachelor's degree in China, I still want to study my major, which is computer science. I believe that in the future computers will be more important and popular. More and more people will work and study in that field. I want to be one of them."

When Bai and her husband return to China, they will be computer software engineers. Their jobs will be good for them because they will get good salaries. Their work will also be good for their country because they will have

a lot of knowledge to share. They will be part of the future of China.

Using the Steps to Write about Your Plans

◆ GETTING IDEAS

THINKING ABOUT YOUR FUTURE

What are your future plans? What will your job be ten years from now? What do you need to study or learn?

FREEWRITING

In your journal, write for three minutes without stopping. Write anything that comes to your mind about your future plans. Don't worry about writing complete sentences. Just keep your pencil moving on your paper!

◆ FOCUSING

Now look at what you wrote. Share your plans with your partner. What is your most important goal? Write a sentence here that states your goal for your future.

Focus: _____

◆ SUPPORTING

Look back at your freewriting to find sentences that explain your main idea, and underline them. Make a list of other information you want to add.

_____

_____

_____

_____

_____

◆ DRAFTING

Now, put your ideas into complete sentences and write your first draft.

_____

_____

_____

_____

_____

_____

_____

_____

_____

_____

_____

_____

_____

_____

_____

_____

_____

◆ REVISING

When you write a composition, it is important to put the ideas in order. For this composition, you should begin with the things that will happen first, and continue to explain things in the order that they will happen. Also, you can help your reader to understand the order of the things you are explaining if you use words such as *first, next, then,* and *finally.*

Exercise 8.1. Putting sentences in the correct order. Arrange the sentences in this composition in a logical order.

My Ambition

(1) My most important goal in life is to shoot animals in Africa, but I won't use a gun. (2) I will use a camera. (3) I am going to finish learning English. (4) I am going to take off for Botswana. (5) I am going to take some courses in photography. (6) I am going to go to college here in the United States. (7) There are many things I need to do before I can begin my career. (8) Because I want to understand all about African animals, I am going to major in biology. (9) I need to find a magazine like *National Geographic* that will pay me for shots of impalas and elephants. (10) This is my dream.

Now insert the word *first* before the first thing that the writer plans to do. Put in the word *next* at the beginning of the sentence that talks about going to college. Add *finally* before the last thing that she plans to do.

REVISING YOUR COMPOSITION

Read your paragraph to a friend. Is there anything he or she wants you to explain about your plans? Next, ask your partner to help you answer these questions about what you wrote. Use your friend's suggestions to help you make changes in your composition.

ORGANIZATION, IDEAS	YES	NO
Is there a main idea sentence that tells what your most important future plan is?		
Do all of the other sentences explain how and why you want to do this?		
Are there enough sentences to make your reader understand what you want to do?		
Are your sentences in a logical order?		
Do some sentences start with words like *next* and *then?*		
Is there a sentence at the end that tells why these plans are important?		

◆ EDITING

CAPITALIZING DAYS AND MONTHS

Days of the week and months of the year always begin with capital letters.

Example: I am going to visit my cousin on Thursday, April 4.

Exercise 8.2. Using capital letters. Put in the necessary capital letters. Remember that proper names of people and places need capital letters, too.

1. we are going to fly to alaska next april.

2. on friday, I am going to have dinner with my friends, mohammed and tom.

3. my husband is going to take a vacation in july and august.

4. can you come to a party at my house on friday night?

5. I am going to arrive in los angeles on tuesday, september 8, at 10:04 a.m.

6. our next soccer game is going to be on saturday afternoon.

7. we are going to go skiing in january and february.

8. next weekend, on saturday and sunday, we are going to go camping.

9. my roommate and I are going to move to a new apartment in august.

10. the students are going to take a trip to california next july.

FUTURE TENSE WITH *GOING TO*

We use *is/am/are going to* + verb to talk about future plans.

SUBJECT	VERB		
I	am	going to	study.
He	is	going to	play.
She	is	going to	go.
It	is	going to	work.
We	are	going to	eat.
You	are	going to	leave.
They	are	going to	come.

Exercise 8.3. Making future sentences. Gloria Glamorous is a famous movie star. Next month she is going to take a vacation. Here is her calendar. Use the information to make *going to* sentences about Gloria.

1. On Monday, February 1, Gloria is going to fly to Aspen.

2. She is going to meet John and ski on Tuesday.

3. _____

4. _____

February

SUNDAY	MONDAY	TUESDAY	WEDNESDAY	THURSDAY	FRIDAY	SATURDAY
	1 fly to Aspen	2 meet John ___ ski	3 have drinks with Kris	4 shop for diamonds	5 go to Liz's party	6 Full Moon fly to Maui
7 relax on the beach	8 have dinner on Tom's yacht	9 surf with Don	10 snorkle	11 dance at the Hilton	12 Abraham Lincoln, 1809 return to L.A.	13 Last Quarter rest
14 St. Valentine's Day go to bed early	15 President's Day	16	17	18	19	20
21 New Moon	22 George Washington, 1732	23	24 Ash Wednesday	25	26	27
28						

January

S	M	T	W	T	F	S
					1	2
3	4	5	6	7	8	9
10	11	12	13	14	15	16
17	18	19	20	21	22	23
24	25	26	27	28	29	30
31						

March

S	M	T	W	T	F	S
	1	2	3	4	5	6
7	8	9	10	11	12	13
14	15	16	17	18	19	20
21	22	23	24	25	26	27
28	29	30	31			

5. _____

6. _____

7. _____

8. _____

9. _____

10. _____

Now fill in this calendar with your plans for next week.

Monday	Tuesday	Wednesday	Thursday	Friday	Saturday	Sunday

Make some sentences about what you and your friends are going to do.

1. _____

2. _____

3. _____

4. _____

5. _____

EDITING YOUR COMPOSITION

Answer the following questions about your composition, and use what you learned in the previous exercises. Correct the grammar, spelling, and punctuation.

GRAMMAR, PUNCTUATION, SPELLING, FORMAT	YES	NO
Do you use the future tense correctly?		
Does every sentence have a capital letter?		
Does every sentence end with a period, question mark, or exclamation point?		
Are the words spelled correctly?		
Is the paragraph indented?		
Is there a heading?		
Is there a title?		

◆ WRITING THE FINAL DRAFT

After you finish revising and editing your composition, write it again.

Using the Steps to Write about the Future

How will our lives be in the year 2025? Where will we live? What kind of transportation will we have? What education will we need? What will we eat?

◆ GETTING IDEAS

MAKING A DIAGRAM

Complete this diagram with your own ideas.

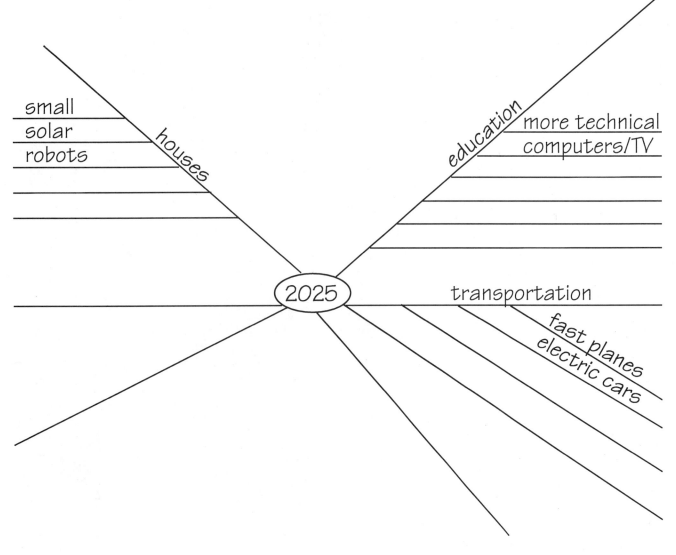

Now share your ideas with your class. Choose someone to put the diagram on the board. Add ideas from the whole class.

◆ FOCUSING

Which part of the diagram has the most ideas? Which thing is interesting to you? Choose *one* topic. For example, do you want to write about travel? What do you want to say about your topic?

Example: Travel in the future will be faster and more convenient, but it will be more expensive.

Now make a sentence with your topic and main idea.

Focus: _____

WRITING SPECIFIC SENTENCES

You need to explain your focus. You have some ideas in your diagram, but you need to make these ideas *specific*. You need to add words to explain exactly and clearly what you mean.

Exercise 8.4. Writing specific sentences. Study the examples below. Rewrite the rest of the sentences so that they are specific.

1. General: People will drive nice cars.

    Specific: <u>People will drive small solar powered electric cars.</u>

2. General: We will eat different kinds of food.

    Specific: <u>We will eat more beans and grains, but there will be less meat.</u>

3. General: Airplanes will travel very fast.

    Specific: _____

4. General: Robots will do many kinds of work.

    Specific: _____

5. General: Cities will be small.

    Specific: _____

6. General: People will travel to some places in outer space.

    Specific: _____

7. General: Clothes will be better.

    Specific: _____

8. General: Schools will have new equipment.

    Specific: _____

9. General: Families will be small.

    Specific: _____

10. General: Doctors will be able to cure some things.

    Specific: _____

Now write some specific sentences about your topic.

_____

_____

_____

_____

_____

_____

_____

♦ DRAFTING

Write your first draft. Use your focus sentence as your first sentence. Use your support sentences from the previous exercise, and add any other information that you need to explain your topic. Write a conclusion that repeats your main idea in different words.

_____

_____

_____

_____

_____

_____

_____

_____

_____

_____

_____

_____

_____

_____

_____

_____

_____

◆ REVISING

Exercise 8.5. Revising a sample composition. The following composition has correct grammar, spelling, and punctuation, but it needs some changes in content and organization. First read the composition. Then follow the suggestions at the end to make changes.

> In the year 2025, I think houses will be apartments because the population will grow very quickly and houses are too big to fit in the space that we will have, so apartments can fit more people living on top of each other. Tall buildings will fill the sky, and fast elevators will carry passengers up and down.
>
> Inside the apartment, rooms will all be open and there will be no big furniture. The kitchen will have fast and safe ovens and refrigerators. The food will last longer and fruit will be bigger and tastier. The television will be important in apartments in the future because people will use it to communicate with other people. For example, we will be able to do all our shopping by television, even for groceries. Also, many people will have television telephones to see the person they are talking to. Finally, I think we will enjoy living in the houses of the future.

1. Give the composition a title.

2. Begin the composition with a main idea sentence that says houses will be small and convenient.

3. Begin the second paragraph with a more general topic sentence.

4. In the sentence that ends ...*no big furniture,* add *such as* and give some examples of big furniture.

5. Take out the sentence that does not really talk about future houses.

135

REVISING YOUR OWN COMPOSITION

Exchange compositions with a partner. Answer these questions about your friend's paper. When you get your own composition back, check your partner's answers. Use them to help you make changes.

ORGANIZATION, IDEAS	YES	NO
Is there a sentence that tells the topic and the main idea?		
Do all the sentences talk about the topic?		
Do all the sentences support the main idea?		
Is the composition interesting?		
Are there specific examples?		
Is the composition at least one page long?		
Is there a conclusion at the end?		

◆ EDITING

FUTURE TENSE WITH *WILL*

We can also use *will* + verb to make the future tense.

> **Examples:** I *will graduate* next June.
> Doctors *will find* a cure for AIDS in the near future.
> **Negative:** People *will not live* on the moon.

Exercise 8.6. Making sentences with will. You want to be the mayor of your town. You are writing a speech to persuade the voters to elect you. Use the words to make sentences promising what you will or will not do when you become mayor.

> **Example:** build/new shopping center
> I will build a new shopping center in our town.

1. repair/all of the streets

137

2. give/the firemen and police/more money

_____

3. construct/a new hospital

_____

4. make/a new city park/with a swimming pool

_____

5. buy/computers/for the schools

_____

6. not/increase/taxes

_____

Now, write sentences making your own promises.

1. _____

2. _____

3. _____

4. _____

Exercise 8.7. Editing a sample composition. This composition is interesting and well organized, but it has some mistakes in grammar and punctuation. Read the composition and follow the directions at the end to make changes.

A Change in Our Food

Our food (be) different in the 2000s in two ways. First, it will be more expensive because we are not taking care of our planet, and we are using up our good land, our trees, and our water. Maybe the food are going to be three times more expensive than now because we not going to have anything in excess.

Second, food will be more healthful. For example, the way to plant the vegetables and fruit will change there will be fewer chemicals, so the fruit and vegetables be more healthful. For this same reason, we are go to have less meat and maybe more chicken. Finally, we are going to have huge changes in the way we eat, and we are going to have to live with them.

1. Follow the example in sentence one. Underline the subject in every sentence and circle every verb.

2. Correct all the mistakes in the verbs.

3. Underline the connecting words *and, but, so, because* twice.

4. Add periods and capital letters to sentences that are joined but do not have a connecting word or correct punctuation.

EDITING YOUR COMPOSITION

Use this checklist to help you correct your composition.

GRAMMAR, PUNCTUATION, SPELLING, FORMAT	YES	NO
Did you use *will* correctly?		
Are the words spelled correctly?		
Does every sentence have a capital letter and a period, question mark, or exclamation point?		
Is the paragraph indented?		
Is there a title?		
Is there a heading?		

♦ WRITING THE FINAL DRAFT

Make all the necessary corrections and then rewrite your composition on another piece of paper.

Going the Extra Mile: Journal Writing

1. You have just won a contest! You will receive a gold credit card to use to buy anything you want, but only for three days. How will you spend the money?

2. Your younger sister is just entering high school, and she is a little afraid. What can you tell her to expect? What advice do you have to give her?

3. Happy New Year! What things are you going to change in your life in the new year?

4. How are you going to spend your next school break?

Appendix

SPELLING REFERENCE LIST

about
again
afternoon
always
are
around
bathroom
because
bedroom
big
black
blue
brother
but
chair
child
children
comfortable
desk
do
does
doesn't
don't
different
eat
eight
evening
every
everyone
family
famous
father
finally
find
first
floor

four
for
friend
from
go
goes
green
hard
has
hear
her
here
him
his
holiday
hotel
hour
house
how
important
interesting
kitchen
know
language
large
left
living room
maybe
many
money
morning
mouth
my
new
night
now

o'clock
orange
other
our
park
people
place
play
put
right
same
says
school
sea
see
short
sister
some
somebody
smoke
study
summer
take
talk
telephone
than
their
them
then
there
these
they
they're
thing
think
third

this
three
tired
to
too
trees
two
vacation
very
water
when
where
which
white
who
winter
with
wonderful
write
wrong
yellow
you
your

DAYS OF THE WEEK

Sunday
Monday
Tuesday
Wednesday
Thursday
Friday
Saturday

MONTHS

January
February
March
April
May
June
July
August
September
October
November
December

141

CORRECTION SYMBOLS

cap	Capital letter	I live in Washington, d.c.
p	Mistake in punctuation	I want milk eggs and bread.
sp	Spelling mistake	Their is a student from Brazil.
agr	Mistake in agreement	He always come late.
wo	Wrong word order	Please come now here.
^	You forgot a word	He my best friend.
wf	Wrong form of word	He walks slow.
tns	Wrong verb tense	In 1980, he lives here.
frag	Incomplete sentence	Because he is tired.
RS	Run-on sentence	I enjoy English I also like to study French.
CS	Comma splice	I enjoy English, I also want to study French.
¶	New paragraph (indent)	

WAYS OF GETTING IDEAS

Brainstorming

Write down any words that come to mind. Limit yourself to 2–3 minutes. Don't stop to talk about the words.

Topic: Friends

FRIENDS

good   believe in you
bad   help you when you're in trouble
like family   everybody needs friends
love   somebody who listens to you
miss my friends   share fun things
hard to find good friends   likes same things

Making a Web or a Map

Write topic in the center. Connect ideas with lines to form a pattern.

Topic: Friends

FRIENDS

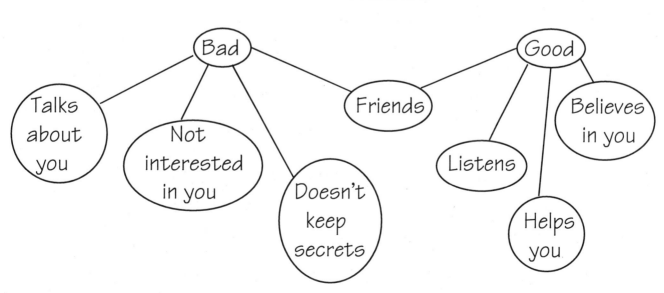

Making a list

This is a good way to show comparison and contrast.

Topic: Friends

Friends

True Friend	False Friend
Gives love	Lies
Believes in you	Tells secrets
Likes same things	Likes you for money or
Shares	other things
Listens	Doesn't keep promises
Helps	

Freewriting

Keep your pencil moving. Write down anything you think of, even if it's not about the topic. Write for 2–3 minutes.

Friends. I like friends, but they're hard to find here in U.S. Why? I don't know. Language? Culture? Who knows. I'm too busy for friends. It takes long time and hard work. What can I say next? Good friend? Who is this? I remember Juan Carlos—a good friend. We played baseball, we talked, we went to parties. We went to school. Had <u>fun</u>!

REVISION AND EDITING GUIDELINES

ORGANIZATION, IDEAS	YES	NO
Is there a sentence that states a main idea?		
Do all other sentences support this main idea?		
Are there enough (6-12 sentences) in each paragraph to develop the main idea?		
Is there a conclusion that ties together the ideas or repeats the main idea?		

GRAMMAR, PUNCTUATION, SPELLING, FORMAT	YES	NO
Is the grammar correct?		
Is the punctuation correct?		
Are words spelled correctly?		
Is each paragraph indented?		
Does each sentence begin with a capital letter and end with a period, question mark, or exclamation point?		
Is there a title, correctly capitalized?		
Is there a heading (name, class, date)?		

0 1 2 3 4 5 6 7 8 9 10

a b c d e f g h i

j k l m n o p q r

s t u v w x y z

A B C D E F G H I

J K L M N O P Q R

S T U V W X Y Z

IRREGULAR PAST TENSE VERB FORMS

Verb	Past
be	was/were
become	became
begin	began
blow	blew
break	broke
bring	brought
buy	bought
come	came
do/does	did
drink	drank
drive	drove
eat	ate
fall	fell
find	found
get	got
give	gave
go/goes	went
grow	grew
have/has	had
hear	heard
know	knew
leave	left
make	made
meet	met
pay	paid
put	put
read	read
run	ran
say	said
see	saw
sit	sat
sleep	slept
speak	spoke
stand	stood
take	took
teach	taught
tell	told
think	thought
understand	understood
win	won
write	wrote

Photo Credits